Handle Gently

An Exploration of a Journey through Grief

By

Wendy Goddard

Copyright © Wendy Goddard 2024

All Rights Reserved

No part of this publication may be reproduced, distributed, or transmitted in any form or by any means, including photocopying, recording, or other electronic or mechanical methods, without the author's prior written permission, except in the case of brief quotations embodied in critical reviews and certain other non-commercial uses permitted by copyright law. For permission requests, please get in touch with the author.

Dedication

This book is dedicated to the memory of Peter, a much-loved husband, father, grandfather, teacher, and friend.

Acknowledgements

My thanks go to my wonderful sons and grandchildren, who kept me going through the darkest hours and without whom this book would never have been written.

I would like to acknowledge the kindness and understanding of my friends who have supported me along this journey. Their encouragement and commitment to keep me connected to the world when I withdrew into silence, has touched me deeply. What is life without precious friendship?

About the Author

Wendy is a mother, grandmother, and great-grandmother and feels that life is going by too quickly. She still keeps busy writing, reading, and researching ideas for whatever project she is working on. Her professional life included nursing, teaching, and eventually retiring from her work as a qualified therapist and trainer.

Handle Gently: An Exploration of a Journey through Grief

Introduction

From too much love of living,
From hope and fear set free,
We thank with a brief thanksgiving
Whatever gods may be
That no life lives forever;
That dead men rise up never;
That even the weariest river
Winds somewhere safe to sea.[1]

This is a book about grief, a book about loss. But it is more than that. It is one person's journey from anguish to acceptance, helplessness to independence, suffering to relief, and melancholy to hope. It is my story after the death of my beloved husband. At least that is what I began with until it grew into a journal of self-exploration – including childhood memories that affected the way I am now and how I dealt with his death; the people in my life that have influenced my progress; and

---

[1] Algernon Charles Swinburne

relationships that have altered the way I think about the world. However, most of all, it is a story of love.

As a teacher and a therapist, I have interwoven my story with theories about grief. For many years, I have been counselling young people and adults who have been left to cope with the multitudinous complications arising from the grieving process. I thought I knew enough to help them. I hope along the way that I have been able to support them in their journey. However, I did not really understand the full impact that loss can have on one's perception of self until my husband died. I had already lost both of my parents. Along the way, I lost a marriage and a baby. I lost my career as a teacher when I lost my health. I was arrogant enough to assume that I knew all about loss. Losing my husband took me into a realm about which I began to find I had no real knowledge. I had experienced some of the emotions in varying degrees, but this time, they were overwhelming, baffling and often almost unbearable.

And so I wrote down my experiences and feelings as a form of personal therapy. I explored the highs and the lows, hoping this would help me through. I realize now that all the highs and lows in my life have influenced the way I have somehow managed to survive this, my greatest loss.

What I have written comes from journal jottings and memories, interlaced with therapeutic thoughts and suggestions that may help others travelling a similar journey. No path we tread will be the same as anyone else's so I can only offer what I have experienced and my reflections.

When we lose some one we love, we are facing new and unmarked territory. We have to start an unplanned journey. This unmapped road has no white lines to guide us; there are no signposts or rules to follow. Sometimes, we move forward and sometimes, we stand still, frozen in a moment of time, one of overwhelming pain, bearing a heavy burden that often seems too hard to carry. Sometimes, we have to travel alone, and sometimes, the journey is shared by others who offer reinforcement, an arm to lean on, a shoulder to cry upon, and they listen quietly as we repeat the same story over and over again.

Perhaps I can be your travelling companion as you travel your road. Maybe a page will make you smile, or a sentence will make you cry. Most of all, I hope you will be encouraged by the fact that I continue to walk a road that is not quite as uphill and treacherous now as it was when I started out. Sometimes, I can even step out briskly towards the sun.

I wish you well on your journey. Travel safely

Wendy Goddard

Chapter 1 Shock and Denial
Before the End

"To regret one's own experiences is to arrest one's development. To deny one's own experiences is to put a lie into the lips of one's own life. It is no less than a denial of the soul."[2]

We sat in the busy car park of the hospital holding, no clutching, each other's hands. We did not speak at first. Both numbed and frozen into silence, we stared into the future through the rain-swept windscreen. Whatever thoughts were going around in our heads I am guessing they were not the same. I sat and quietly panicked, trying to get myself together so that I could support Peter. I have no doubt that he was looking at the news we had received scientifically, practically and, as usual, with little emotion so that he could provide me with his familiar rational observations.

When he eventually spoke, he informed me that his mother had had leukaemia and lived to ninety-six. His voice was eerily calm.

---

[2] Oscar Wilde, De Profundis

Almost lightly, he said he felt far too well to be really ill, although he admitted that he was more tired than he used to be. But at eighty - one what should one expect? He emphasized that his mother had all her faculties when she died and that it was not leukaemia that killed her in the end.

I tried to ask him how he felt about the diagnosis, but all he said was that he had had a good life and that if this was to be the beginning of the end, then so be it. He did not believe that the doctors could really predict what would happen. He repeated that he felt fit and well and anyway when the time was right, we would go together as we had always planned. I did not believe these were his honest reactions, but I knew better than to question him about his feelings. He had always followed his body and would go to the doctor whenever he felt something was wrong. He had a faith in science that did not exist in other matters, such as religion or matters of the heart. He had, after all, gone to the doctor this time as soon as he felt something was not quite right. Luckily, his doctor, a young man in whom he had great faith, had evidently taken him seriously enough to order a blood test. And now here we were collecting the results and the prognosis.

I knew then that we were both dealing with shock at the news.

We went and bought fish and chips and sat in the car beside the beautiful harbour, watching the windsurfers. This was a place we used to come so often to watch the sunset - Evening Hill – such a lovely name for a beautiful view. It was always full of active windsurfers, boats, and ships entering the deeper harbour of Poole. This was the place where he had patiently walked beside me slowly up the hill after my hip operations, trying to improve the strength in my legs; a place where we would sit and discuss where we would go on our next travels when I was healed. Now, we did not talk about travel. In fact, I do not think we talked of anything very much. I thought about the evening of our lives drawing in and how we might spend the time, we had left together, however long that may be.

Neither of us really wanted to believe that there was anything seriously wrong. This was just a blood disease that he could live with, and maybe he would have to be a bit more careful about not overtiring himself, but we could manage it together. It seemed impossible that I had been through four major operations and survived and that he should be the one who would succumb to cancer.

We discussed practical ways to make life easier and slower. At that time, he was still riding his bike to the shops and the allotment, spending much of his days keeping the vegetable plots productive. At some point, it had struck me that they were not as kempt and up to scratch as they used to be, but I did not say anything because I did not want to seem as though I was criticizing him in what was, after all, his main interest in life. Much later, I found a birthday letter among his effects that he had written to me in which he had said that his main joy in life was growing vegetables. Peter was a simple soul who needed very little, whose footsteps on the earth were light, and who was pleased by the ordinary little gifts that life bestowed upon him. Who was I to comment on what seemed a lack of effort? Little did I realize it was actually because he was so tired. He was sleeping longer in the afternoons, but I did not think anything was wrong, merely increasing age and I even used to tease him about his 'old man' siestas.

We had Christmas ahead and a family gathering to organize. I know he did not enjoy all the fuss at this time of year, but he loved having the family gatherings. We did not know that it would be his last Christmas. Would I have done anything differently? I doubt it. There are no special presents you can give to a man when you know he is dying except the gift of life, and that was not in my power to give. As I write this, I regret not asking whether a bone marrow or stem cell transplant would have helped. Maybe we did ask, but I cannot remember and I am sure we would have pursued this if it could have been done. Or maybe we both felt that the doctors would not consider it because of his age.

I remember at some point during the festivities, after presents had been opened and the meal had been enjoyed, we sat and listened to my son playing his guitar. I looked at Peter lying back in the recliner with a small smile on his face and his eyes shut. I suddenly thought, "He may not be here next year. How will I cope without him?" But I quickly dismissed the thought as I watched him because he looked so well, peaceful, indestructible, and utterly content surrounded by family and grandchildren. Content was a word he often used to describe himself when, like most women do when seeking reassurance, I asked him if he was happy. He was not a man to have highs and lows. His emotions remained on an even keel. That is why he was always my rock. When I was anxious, he would put my mind at rest, and when I fretted about the children, he would remind me that they were adults and had their own lives to run and their own decisions to make.

January came and we had to visit the hospital again for the next blood test results. We were directed to the Oncology department. The waiting room was very busy and sitting near to us was a woman in tears, her husband talking quietly to her. I remarked to Peter how awful to have news of your impending demise and to have to sit in a public waiting room. We guessed that she was the one who was dying because she had on a hat to cover her baldness. Not once did I really think that Peter was about to receive the same news. I remember thinking how lacking in privacy it seemed to have to sit in a cold, soulless waiting room.

The consultant was very gentle and informed us that the Leukaemia had transmuted into Acute Myeloid Leukaemia, a cancer of the white blood cells. She explained that there was very little that could be done and that the condition would progress rapidly and aggressively. Immediate treatment might delay the end but would not be a cure.

That was when our lives really began to change. Had she known this before Christmas? Had they saved the news until the festivities were over? What questions did we need to ask?

The choices we had seemed to be few. We could let nature take its course, or we could go for a combination of chemotherapy and blood transfusions, the first to kill off the cancer cells and the second to keep him topped up with healthy blood, hoping that this would eventually replace the cancerous cells. However, this meant that Peter would have to start the treatment in the hospital so that everything could be kept sterile because he would be vulnerable to infection. Interestingly, that was the only place he later caught any infections.

We were warned of the side effects of the treatments and given leaflets to take away to help us with our decision. It was hard to take in all the details. So we were sent away to discuss what treatment we wanted, but the truth was that Peter had very little time left.

I can still hear him talking to the consultant and telling her that he could not possibly be dying. He said he felt far too well. He was just tired. I do not know if this was fear, denial or reality. But at this point, I knew what she was saying was true and my only hope then was to keep him with me and pain-free as long as I could. The doctor pronounced that, without treatment, it would be a few weeks at most.

With treatment, he might have an extra few months, perhaps until March. As I re-read this I remember the question Peter asked her, "Is it anything I have done that has caused this?" As though he could have done anything to bring about such a devastating disease. He did not smoke, drank very little, the odd glass of wine maybe, and always kept himself fit and full of energy, running everywhere. Later, we discussed the number of people on our road who had had cancer, and we began to think it was the mobile phone antennae on the local fire station tower which overlooked our gardens that caused this. He thought it may have been his love of the sun, but he had always taken care using creams and avoiding sunburn. We laughingly recalled the visit to Australia when he used to stand and rotate himself slowly in the sun, determined to tan every part of his body and the many times on our travels he had searched for naturist beaches where he could sunbathe. But in the end, he accepted that it was not the sun but that it was merely 'unfortunate' that he happened to have pulled the short straw.

Yet again, we found ourselves in the hospital car park armed with the information from which we would have to decide how to proceed. I had a huge lump in my throat that I knew could burst at any moment. I asked Peter if he wanted to go anywhere, but he replied that he just wanted to go home.

We drove away from the hospital in painful silence. I did not know what to say, and I think he was too shocked to even try to make sense of it all this time. I tried not to cry. I felt I had to be strong for him. I was imagining what it must feel like to be told that your life would soon end and somehow could not find any words of comfort. Instead, I felt selfish for imagining what my life would be like without Peter in it. We do not prepare ourselves for such events and I found myself unable to find the words to speak to someone faced with their own mortality. Somehow, it was so different from counselling a stranger and seldom have I felt so inadequate as a comforter. I remember the fear I felt - fear of losing him, fear of not being able to talk about the things that mattered, fear of being alone, and fear of what was to come.

I began to panic as I felt my carefully organized life unravelling. I have never done chaos well and I have always found it hard to cope with change that is forced upon me. I knew that I could cope as I had done before, but it would be with an enormous struggle. I have compartmentalized my life and my home.

I spend hours working in my office upstairs, overlooking the school playing fields. I relish the time I spend there. Sometimes, I gaze out of the window and as I watch the foxes at play in the field and later enjoy the children running and tumbling, almost mirroring the activities of the family of foxes, I feel total contentment.

When I take a break from my clients or from writing and researching, I head for my workroom or the conservatory to engage in more creative activities. During the day, when we are together we plan outings, evening meals and holidays and share our thoughts and our memories. Or we sit and read, Peter with his science fiction and me with the latest thriller. We always have supper together even though we rarely sit down at the same time for other meals. He enjoys being my sous chef and I happily invent meals for the two of us. When he is at the allotment, I keep myself busy, barely missing him. At night, we retire together more or less at the same time because we both like to read in bed.

We enjoy relaxing together. Our lives are fairly structured, but we take time out to go for walks, pub lunches, and visits to gardens. Our independent lives are so intertwined that there is scarcely a moment when we do not consider the other. Peter is always there for me in the background when I am working. I remember all those buffet lunches he prepared for the participants of my training groups. At times, I can call on him when I am having trouble with the technology or commandeer him to laminate my training materials. When I want to talk through the day's training, he listens patiently and encouragingly, and when I train abroad, he happily accompanies me, organizing the tickets and hotels. I feel that Peter is ever at my side. Sometimes, on long summer days I go and sit and watch him work on his allotment or in the garden. Occasionally, I help pick the fruit or weed the beds, but mostly, I enjoy just being with him.

We travel widely together. We help raise our grandchildren together. Although we have different tastes in reading and television and sometimes in music, on the whole we share most pleasures. Our lives are companionable, loving and relaxed. We talk often of how we would die together because although I am twelve years younger than him, he is the healthier one and his family was longer living than mine. Neither of us wants to outlive the other. We are content in the life we have built for ourselves and neither of us can imagine continuing without the other.

I remember when Peter went to a talk presented by Dignitas and we had long conversations about euthanasia, suicide and the ethics involved. Neither of us wants to be a burden to anyone, and we could not foresee a time when one would outlive the other.

Suddenly, all this was going to change. We are now faced with a new version of how it would be.

Peter is going to die and I would have to carry on without him. How do you discuss this without seeming selfish and self-centred? How do you ask a man who knows he is dying to help you solve all the practical problems before he goes? How do you talk about funeral arrangements, bodies, and life or no life after death? How do you fill your remaining days when one has a death sentence and the other has a life sentence? What do you tell the children and grandchildren? How do you discuss finances with someone who has helped to save it but won't be there to spend it?

Wendy Goddard

All these thoughts raced around my head in the next few hours while Peter was resting and in the end, I knew that the only way I would survive the coming weeks or months would be to keep as much control over the event as I could. I knew too, that the only way that he would be able to deal with it was to have everything as normal as possible and for him to retain his independence for as long as he could.

Thoughts

1. Keep an ongoing list of any questions, however mundane or stupid they might seem. And ensure that you get answers. If necessary, write down the answers because it is easy to forget them in a heightened state of emotion. I started a notebook in which I wrote whatever queries we had ready to ask when we went back to the consultant.

2. "God laughs when we make plans" – But continue to plan as though life will go on because it will for you.

3. Take control over what you can as soon as you can. Being out of control is one of the greatest causes of depression. In illness, we need to take back control wherever we can.

4. Think through such matters as finances and the funeral and be ready to discuss them when the time seems right. And there will be times when the one who is dying may be able and willing to talk about these things.

Wendy Goddard

Chapter 2 Anger
Nearing the End

Anger is one letter short of danger.[3]

We began to plan our days ahead. Peter had to have transfusions on a regular basis to try to counteract the cancerous cells. We had decided a first dose of chemotherapy would perhaps give him longer provided that it did not make him ill. We were both aware of the side effects but he wanted to try it and see if it would help. I regret this decision more than any other, as this was the only time that he became really poorly. It pulled him down so much that, for the first time, he actually had to face the fact that he was dying. Being in hospital for ten days was a terrible time for both of us and certainly, those were the worst days of the remaining months we had together. Those days of sickness, pain and confusion were by far the hardest to bear. At one stage, when I sat by his bedside, he said quietly, "I am ready to

---

[3]Author Unknown

go now!" But I refused to let him give up. This was not his time. We still had precious days ahead.

When he got an infection from the central line, I was so angry. The one place you expect to be safe is in the care of nursing staff in a hospital. He became quite delirious for a while and desperately wanted to come home, but they would not allow it because they said he was too ill. All I could think of was that he wasn't ill before he entered the hospital. He was not ill before they started treatment. I stayed by his side every day. But each night, as I had to leave him and drive home to an empty house I knew that I was leaving him alone and could not be sure what was happening to him. Were the nurses watching over him? Were they giving him water when he wanted it? Would they move his pillows so that he was more comfortable? I hated the thought that he was alone and suffering.

I spent a lot of this time remembering how we had found each other.

Peter had been my friend and my Head of Department in a boys' secondary school for about eight years before he retired, and I managed to obtain his job. He was so different from many of the teachers there: 'a perfect gentleman' as he was so often described, and being in quite a macho environment, it was a lovely change to work with someone who had respect for women. When I finally moved on to another school as a Deputy Head, I invited him to a leaving party held in my garden. I had expected him to come with his wife, but he came alone and during the evening he explained that she had left him when he retired. All those years and he had never mentioned it. Years of popping into school to see me after his retirement and I thought he had been checking up on me to see how I was managing to do his old job. Instead it appeared that he had been trying to find an opportunity to ask me out, unable to do so because he thought I may be with someone else. When my son pointed out at the party that he thought he fancied me, I laughed and said that we had known each other for years as colleagues and that I had always thought of Peter as my boss.

We married in July a year later and honeymooned in France. Peter said he would never leave me again.

A poem written by a friend for Peter's Condolence book sums up our love.

"Of course, Peter came to your house for a barbeque and never left. He had found his Wendy. He still searched his maps, but really didn't need to go any farther than his garden except for the occasional adventure to somewhere new like Clonmell, where I was lucky enough to meet him." Karen Wingett

Often, I would introduce us to others as a couple as Peter and Wendy as in Peter Pan. They rarely forgot our names after that introduction. How well we went together.

Peter took dancing lessons so that he could invite me to a 'Friends of the Earth' Dinner Dance, our first date. He was not a natural dancer, but he knew how much I liked it. This gesture was so typical of his character: providing pleasure for others, even if not for himself. And yet he said he was not a romantic.

Going home to an empty house when Peter was in hospital, I would wonder whether he would ever come back to me. I could not relax and sleep eluded me most nights. I walked around the house feeling its emptiness. Through endless cups of tea and meaningless television programmes, I tried to pass the time until I could return to him.

Looking back at this time, I realize how much anger I felt and I directed it towards the staff who I thought had let us down. The infection in Peter's central line must have been because they did not sterilise the needle. The transfusion when the blood ran under the skin of his arm instead of into a vein was sheer carelessness on the part of a nurse who failed to check on him when the buzzer sounded the fifteen-minute check time. His arm swelled up like a rugby ball and the bruising this caused stayed with him until he died months later. The chemotherapy made him so sick that he wanted to die. All of these things were in the control of someone else and I blamed them for Peter's distress. Of course, I did not express this anger but pushed it down inside me to support him. It certainly would not have helped to have been overtly angry with the staff.

We stopped the chemotherapy after that first round and when they finally managed to bring his temperature down, he was allowed home. The doctor insisted that if it went up again, I was to take him back to the hospital immediately. We talked about this and Peter said that, whatever happened, he did not want to go back. I had to take his temperature night and morning and lived in fear of its rising, but I knew that should that happen, we would deal with it together at home. From then on it was strict barrier nursing and we decided we would fight whatever happened together in a place of safety where I could control the environment.

With all the precautions we took, Peter's temperature stayed down.

With no ability to combat infections, I controlled the home environment to such an extent that he began to regain his strength and vitality. Everything was sterilized. A notice on the front door requested people not to visit if they had an infection. I supplied bacterial gel and masks. No one would get away with not using them! It became second nature to keep the home as sterile as possible. Plants were thrown out, flowers banned, and antiseptic gel met each visitor as they entered. I washed raw food in Milton, and made sure that Peter had the diet they recommended. Even when we had to go to the hospital for blood transfusions, I stayed with him to make sure that such precautions were followed. No one was allowed near him if they had an infection and even the doctors and care team had to follow the instructions.

Peter wanted to die at home. I was determined that he would have his wish, although at this time, I am not sure I really believed that he was going to die. He looked so much better and he was still going up and down stairs and engaging with life.

At the time, I did not really consider what dying at home might entail. We were suddenly surrounded by a wonderful team of people who seemed almost to anticipate our every wish. The doctor had held our Living Wills for some time and he promised that whatever happened, he would honor Peter's request not to be resuscitated. In time, we were given the end of life kit, which although hidden from him, enabled me to reassure him that he would not be allowed to suffer. Gradually, as the weeks passed, various items would be supplied that Peter needed for home care.

I knew the days ahead would be challenging, having watched over both my parents as they died. I had sat alone with my father as he died of cancer in the Macmillan Unit. I had watched the life drain away, talking to him until his final breath. The care he had received had been excellent. Fortunately, my father had only been in the unit during his last few days, but I remember thinking how sad it was that he had never been able to appreciate the drinks trolley coming round in the evening! He would have liked that bit of luxury. But I had had an opportunity to administer to him in those last days and to be with him when he died.

Wendy Goddard

My mother died subsequently in a nursing home after long years of gradually leaving us as her memories faded and her mobility became restricted by a series of strokes. Every day, I would visit her and make sure she ate her lunch. The grandchildren were small then but they too would come in to see her even though she did not really know who they were. I sat beside her at the end and repeated the goodbyes that had been said through those painful years. I was saddened by both deaths, but those people I knew and loved were no longer really present and their deaths were a release for them and for me. And both deaths took place in safe places where there were staff around to support me. I was very afraid that I would not be able to do things right for Peter.

This time, I was to be with him at home as he slowly left me, a man to whom I had given my heart late in life. After twenty years of marriage and many years before that, as friends and colleagues, he had become my best friend as well as my love. Peter was my mentor, my champion, my rock. It was to him that I took my troubles and Peter that I had followed into unknown territory. I trusted him with my life, at times quite literally, when travelling in strange places.

As the few weeks we had been given became extended, we made the most of them. We visited a few of his favorite places in the first month often just sitting in the car watching sunsets or taking short walks along the beach. We went to Bradbury Rings and Kimmeridge, across the Avon Valley and to Stockley to feed the fish, and one day we drove through Hardy's Dorset identifying the places written about in his books. When Peter became too weak and lost interest in going out in the car, we spent precious time together talking, reading and reminiscing.

In our own surroundings he was able to be comfortable and choose for himself what to do and when. He could read or listen to the radio all night without disturbing others. He could sleep all day without being woken up to take his medication. He could decide what he wanted to eat and at what time.

When the hospital bed was delivered, he became very angry and refused to use it on the first night. I think the reality of why he had been provided with such a bed made him realize that he was not going to recover. When he discovered how comfortable it was and that with its wooden headboard, it did not look like a hospital bed, he seemed quite happy to settle into it. The recliner chair near the patio window gave him a place to sit and listen to his music. Having the bathroom on the same level meant that he could still use it while he was able to do so and he struggled with this as long as he could, using a walking frame or being wheeled to it. When he could no longer do so, it was convenient for me to see to his personal care without going up and down the stairs. I slept in our bedroom with the door open between us so that I could see and hear him at night.

After years of being kept awake by his snores, I can now remember the comfort of hearing him during those nights. It meant that he was still with me. But those long dark nights were hard. I was on constant alert and fearful of when the end would come, not really knowing how it would come. I wished that I had been able to ask the questions: "what will it be like?" "How will I know when he is actually dying?" But I couldn't then. It would have been too real, a sign of my acceptance of Peter's death, and I did not want to reach that stage. Even though I had been with my parents, I knew that every death was different. I looked up Cheyne Stokes breathing but even that did not help me to recognize the signs in those final hours.

Meanwhile, Peter's dignity was maintained. I nursed him and cared for him until I could no longer do so. In the last three days, when he drifted into unconsciousness, I was unable to lift him and the palliative care came in to provide nursing support. Everything I needed was supplied by them. They arranged the bed, chair, commode, bottles and so much more. They sent a sitter for a couple of hours each week to let me go out to shop. Family and friends came in to relieve me to get my hair done or go for a beach walk. The oncology nurse kept close contact making sure we were both well prepared and knew whom to contact at all times should we need to do so, and she acted as liaison with the hospital, GP and district nurses. I felt I was not alone in this, although at times I desperately needed some space to myself away from encroaching death. My world shrank to the size of my home and finally, in that last week, to the size of the room in which we shared our last days together.

Handle Gently: An Exploration of a Journey through Grief

When I first started to write this journal, Peter was already slipping away from me. He had been through twenty-seven audio books by Terry Pratchett, which, fortunately, he did not ask me to read to him. I was extremely disappointed when I did not receive a reply from the author to my letter telling him how those books had sustained us, how much I had enjoyed hearing my husband's laughter and seeing his pleasure at having another book to listen to when I returned from the library. Then I found out that the author had been having to cope with his own illness and I forgave him knowing how awful Alzheimer's must be for a man who used language to give such pleasure to others.

Later, when it became too difficult to concentrate on the audio books, Peter asked me to read "Fortunes of War" to him. I found this very comforting because it would take so long to read it all. I was already beginning to bargain with death. "Give me time to read this book, all three volumes, and then you can take him", thinking that would give us at least another month.

As I read, I stopped every now and again to remind him of the places we had been, things we had seen, memories brought back by the book: the peace of the lakeside cafe in Riga in snowfall, the decorated elephants at a Sikh wedding we attended in India; feeding the beautiful tropical fish while snorkelling in Tahiti; strolling through the night market in Singapore; Peter's ascent up Ayres Rock while I read all the caution signs and anxiously observed the crosses on the side; New Year's Eve under a full moon on the backwaters of Kerala on a converted rice barge; the unforgettable experience of Auschwitz and visiting the salt mines at Wieliczka. I pinned photos around his bed and we talked about the times we had shared. Some days I cried, but on others, I could smile and laugh and feel hope for the future. I knew that when Peter finally left me, I would be lost for a while and that life would never be the same without him. But I knew I would feel no guilt. I would have done everything needed to provide him with the death he had wanted.

On his final Saturday night, he became extremely agitated. With an angry desperation, he kept trying to get out of bed, climbing over the guardrail and clawing up the wall. I was terrified that he would hurt himself, and for an hour or so, we struggled together. He kept saying how strong I was, but I did not feel it. I talked softly and calmly to him, trying to explain that if he hurt himself now, he would end up back at the hospital and would probably not be able to come back home. After all, we had been through together, was this really worth the risk? Gradually, he calmed down and fell into a deep sleep.

When I called the team the next morning, they came straight out. Those desperate attempts had been the last stages of activity of the brain fighting for life. They said I should have called them and they could have given Peter something to calm him. Looking back, I know they would have come even though it was in the middle of the night, but somehow, we needed to go through this last struggle together. He knew that I was there for him in those last terrifying moments of consciousness. After they gave him an injection on Sunday morning, he never regained consciousness, and slowly the life drained away during the last few days.

As I sat and watched over Peter, I felt honored to have been able to give back some of the care and love that he had shown me during our years together. I acquired an inner strength, an ability to live in the moment, and most of all patience. I do not regret one moment of this time, even though my life had been on hold for six months. I knew that when the end came, it would be hard to bear, but after that final struggle, I so wanted him to be at peace. I would be with him when he left this world the way he had lived in it: peacefully, calmly, quietly, with great dignity and surrounded by love.

I know how lucky we have been. I have learned so much from this experience. One of the greatest fears must be to die alone and in pain. I could not allow that to happen to Peter whatever it took. And maybe, out of this, I can offer support to others who have to die alone. Who knows?

Thoughts

1. Never leave unsaid those things that need to be said. I cherished the time we had to talk about everything. There were things that I needed to share with Peter, even though at times it was hard to say them. Knowing that this was the last chance I had made every conversation so very important.

2. Speak out if something appears to be wrong. Medical staff do make mistakes and unless their attention is brought to those concerns, they cannot deal with them.

3. I realized that there were important times like this in my life when I could tell friends I did not want to see them. If I have lost any, I am sad, but I also feel real friends are there for you even if you lose touch and withdraw for a while.

4. Try to hang on to memories and name them. I think it was so important to share those memories with Peter, and he often said what a full life he had had with me. It was an affirming time for both of us to review the life we had shared together.

5. I know that many people do not get the opportunity I had and that their loved ones are taken suddenly or they are unable to be with them at the end. Someone said to me, "At least you had time to say goodbye." Her husband had died suddenly of a heart attack. At the time, I felt quite angry with her because she seemed to assume her grief was more painful than mine. Everyone grieves differently, and each feels the

pain on a different level. I am learning to be compassionate with those who make careless remarks out of their own sense of loss.

6. Maybe we need to be more prepared for our own demise. We never know when it may come. I have been able to write a detailed account of my finances, my funeral arrangements, and what to do regarding probate and where my children can find all my papers. I included a list of people who may want to be informed of my death. These practical preparations may help my family when my time comes.

7. Find out as much as you can about what the end of life may entail so that families are prepared. I was totally unprepared for that final struggle.

Wendy Goddard

Chapter 3 Despair
The Dying of the Light.

"Out of my nature has come wild despair; an abandonment to grief; anguish that wept aloud; misery that could find no voice; sorrow that was dumb..." [4]

The true grieving process starts when the reality of death is upon us. I had not been prepared for the devastation of the loss I was about to experience. I had tried to imagine the things I could do when the waiting was over, the places I would go, the relief of not having to keep a vigil any longer. These thoughts sustained me during those final hours, but in a way, they were my denial of the reality of his death.

When Peter finally left me, I was holding him in my arms. He took a few very slow breaths and then stopped breathing. A few minutes later, it seemed he took a last deep breath. I almost believed it had all been a terrible dream and that he was not going to die after all. Maybe that deep breath was the beginning of a healing process.

---

[4] Oscar Wilde : De Profundis

I began to cry with the realization that I was fooling myself, and he had finally stopped breathing. A teardrop traced its way down his cheek as though he had heard my cry, and he was crying for me. I had never seen him cry before, and this one teardrop broke my heart.

Mahler's Fifth Symphony played quietly, and candles were lit around his bed. I had massaged him with sweet oils and spoken to him gently about it being his time now – time to let go.

> *As I bathe you with these aromatic oils*
>
> *And lightly stroke your beauty*
>
> *In loving you and celebrating*
>
> *Your fading life energy*
>
> *I am graced with being reborn*
>
> *Into a life without you.*

But as his light went out, so too did mine. I did not feel as though I had been graced with being reborn. I did not realize then that it would take so long to rekindle a spark within me. This grief I felt as he died was like no other I had ever experienced. I felt my heart breaking as I drowned his body with tears.

I felt halved, not only in my very being but in everything I could do or could accomplish. He was my adviser, my support, my sounding board, my best friend, my one true love. I sat with him sobbing uncontrollably. I felt such pain of loss that I was sure I would never be the same again.

The next two hours, waiting for the doctor and the funeral directors, I sat by him until he was cold. I laid out his clothes for him to wear to his funeral. Even though no one would see him, I knew he would want to be dressed in his comfortable white kurta bought in India and his little Moroccan hat that he wore around the house to keep his head warm. I watched the van that carried his body away and my sobs were uncontainable. I knew that this was the last time he would leave the home we had shared and that he would never return to me. I had made the decision that I did not want to see him laid out at the funeral home. I had seen him lying in peace in his bed, which was enough. I had said my goodbyes.

As I think about that moment of his departure, I am reminded of a time in my youth when I was sent away to a boarding school in Buckinghamshire. I was only seven or eight years old and my parents had believed that a boarding school education was the best for myself and my brothers. I hated the school, which seemed so big and impersonal, where older girls could bully the newbies and get away with it. I remember standing at the window as my parents drove away and the feeling of total abandonment that came over me. A cruel sense of injustice overwhelmed me, and I was so angry with them. And at that moment, I hated them for their heartlessness. I stood for a long while with my forehead pressed against the window, tears streaming down my face. I do not remember anyone coming to comfort me or to explain why this was happening to me.

As Peter was taken away from me, I felt that same sense of abandonment and injustice. There was no one to blame, but I felt powerless and defenceless at that moment. No one could offer me comfort because the only person who could understand my pain was the one leaving me behind. However many arms there were to encircle me, they were not his arms. Whatever voices spoke words of solace, they were not his voice. Eventually, exhausted I slept while my family stayed to watch over me. I longed with all my heart for it all to be a dream – that I would awake and find that he was lying beside me, comforting me in my nightmare vision of hell. Because surely that is what it would be like, a living hell to survive him. Not to be able to laugh with him over some silly private joke we shared, not to be able to watch the intent expression on his face as he made love to me, not to be able to follow him into unknown places guided by his treasure trove of maps; not to be able to watch him planting his carefully nurtured seeds into the soil of his allotment; No longer to see his gentle smile as he watched our grandchildren grow – this indeed was a nightmare.

I did not even see the grief of the family. I was too wrapped up in my own to realize that there were others who would be missing him and grieving his loss. I needed to be alone with his smell still on the pillow and his dressing gown wrapped around me for comfort. There was no room in my heart at that time to comfort others.

Thoughts

1. Whatever our expectations of death may be it still takes us by surprise. Each person leaves the world differently, and each of us experiences that loss in our own unique manner. No amount of preparation emotionally can ever be enough for that final moment when death comes.

2. Weep tears for your beloved. There is no one at the end who is more important than you and the one for whom you grieve. There will be time enough to support others who mourn the departed. Allow yourself time to do your own mourning in private if that is want you want.

3. Communicate with the loved one before death and afterwards. We do not know how long they sense our presence when they are dying. Our touch and our voices maybe so precious to them in those moments. And if the soul, the spirit or the being takes a while to depart the body after the breath ceases, what better way to say farewell than by talking, singing, or praying. According to Tibetans, after death, the consciousness takes at least 49 days to travel from one life to the next.

4. Do not fear death. The passing into whatever lies beyond (whether nothingness or another life) is not to be feared. At the last moment, there is only peace.

5. The ideal for the dying person is to be with family in the intimacy of home. Dying is part of living. A precious time of opportunity. A loving time, and a time for deepening relationships, a time for sharing wisdom, for trusting and reconciling, for forgiving. I know that many will not have this opportunity, but may be faced with a shared ward in a clinical environment with merely curtains to protect their privacy. Others may have to face a sudden death. However it comes, I think that we all have to find our way through the process of grieving.

Wendy Goddard

Chapter 4
The Funeral

Stop all the clocks, cut off the telephone,

Prevent the dog from barking with a juicy bone,

Silence the pianos and with muffled drum

Bring out the coffin, let the mourners come.[5]

I do not remember well the days between Peter's death and the funeral. I know that my family was around me, that arrangements had to be made, and that life had to go on.

Peter had already chosen his special music. In the last weeks, when he was still able to go out in the car, we visited his favorite countryside spots. One evening, we were sitting in the car watching a beautiful sunset over the Purbecks and eating our picnic tea, though his meal consisted of only a nutritious drink by this time. We began to talk about the music we enjoyed. I asked him if he was stranded on a desert island and which pieces he would choose. He

---

[5] W.H.Auden

began in his practical way, saying that it would be unlikely that a music player of any kind would survive. We didn't talk much about the actual funeral since he had already expressed the view that very few people would be interested and thus, a small affair would suffice. If he had only known! But he knew I would want it to be perfect and so, guessing what I was doing, he did not prevent me from collating his choices.

He chose Richard Strauss' "Four Last Songs",; "None but the Lonely Heart" by Tchaikovsky; "When I am Laid in Earth" by Purcell from Dido & Aeneas and Mahler's Fifth Symphony. It was so obvious he knew what I was doing and why I had asked the question because the pieces of music were so appropriate. But he often listened to these so I knew too that they were among his favourites. I wrote his eulogy while he was dying, and I had read it to him while he lay unconscious in those last hours. I like to believe he had heard it and knew how much I loved him.

Peter, my love, my friend,

'Was my North, my South, my East and West

My working week and my Sunday rest,

My noon, my midnight, my talk, my song;

I thought that love would last forever; I was wrong.'[6]

---

[6] W.H.Auden

Peter was my soul mate, my best friend, and my partner through twenty years of love, laughter and tears. He took me to places I would never have gone alone: down forbidden tracks and exploring dangerous roads into the majestic wilderness and crowded cities. He was an explorer, an adventurer, and a navigator. He could find his way out of a strange town by the way it was constructed, not just by reading a map. We seldom got lost, and if we did, it never mattered. He was always calm always gentle as he put us back on track.

Confusion rarely came except when navigating by the sun in the southern hemisphere. He was so certain we were heading in the right direction, and even though our fuel was running low, he refused to turn around. Unfortunately, he had forgotten that the world was upside down!

In our years together, we had a few disagreements but only one major argument and that took place in Calico when he wanted to leave the tourist town, and I wanted to stay and see the cowboys fight at the OK Corral and pan for gold in the river. I wanted to enjoy the fun. Peter was not a "fun" sort of guy, even though he enjoyed life to the full.

Always willing to do what I wanted to do or go where I wanted to go (with that one exception). He always put others' needs before his own. He believed his purpose in life was to serve others. And he did…… *from silver service on a P&O ship to teaching unwilling boys in school.*

He was the problem solver and the inventor. His constructions on the allotments were not things of beauty, but they worked. He kept anything and everything that might have a future use. He was a recycler before it became popular, measuring water into a kettle and conserving the heat in a thermos flask. Never run a hot tap if cold water would do. Altering the heating and thinking I would not notice the chill.

I enjoyed rebelling against his little foibles and he never got angry.

He took care of me, supported me and guided me gently and lovingly through some difficult times with my health. He was truly my navigator, my pilot.

It was a privilege and an honor to care for him when he needed me most. He accepted dying the way he had accepted life: calmly, philosophically, peacefully, quietly and with great dignity, surrounding himself with love. He was a true gentleman. And to misquote one of his favorite authors, Ray Bradbury.

When he died, I suddenly realized I wasn't crying just for him at all but for the things he did. I cried because he would never do them again: he would never dig in his allotment or show the grandchildren the stars or play the violin the way he once did, or find an answer to every question he was asked. He was part of us and when he died, all the actions stopped dead, and there was no one to do them the way he did. He was an individual. He was an important man. I will never get over his death. He shaped our world. He did things to our world. The world was bankrupted of ten million fine actions the night he passed on.

But Auden was wrong. Love does last forever. The loved never really dies, for love is immortal. He will walk beside me forever in my heart, and he will forever be navigating my safe passage."

The excellent funeral directors had enabled us complete freedom to organize everything the way we wanted them. My sons produced a magnificent coffin made from recycled pallets and, as a committed recycler and energy saver, Peter would have approved of this, his final resting place. The grandchildren spent an afternoon together stencilling the polished box with the words "Handle Gently", "This Way Up", and "Fragile". That session became a lovely way for them to say goodbye and honor the memory of Grandpa. They shared their tears and their laughter, the mistakes that were made with the spellings, and the gentle chidings and corrections made by their peers. They talked about their grandfather as they decorated the coffin, sharing fond memories and funny stories and – creating a bank of stored wisdom they had inherited from him.

My eldest grandson, training to work in the woodland, rescued a piece of oak and made a memorial plaque carved with Peter's name and dates. It stands today in my conservatory, and though the carved name has faded with time and sun, just as his image is no longer as sharp and clear today in my mind, the memories are still stronger and, indeed growing even more vibrant as I write this.

My daughter-in-law, a teacher and potter, created an urn in the shape of a beehive in memory of Peter's beekeeping days, and the urn still stands in his shed, though empty now of his ashes.

At the end of the funeral, each person filed out passed Peter's coffin and laid a single flower upon it, some touching it gently, others bowing before it in homage to the gentle man gone forever. My son played his guitar quietly in the background until everyone had left.

Five of our seven grandchildren read the final prayer between them. I had chosen it to suit everyone, believer or atheist. The Great Invocation is intended to be used by all. The use of the name Christ as it appears in the Invocation is not a limitation of spiritual understanding but an expansion. Christ is known as the World Teacher, and he is that great being known to Buddhists as the Lord Maltreya and by Muslims as Imam Mahdi. "Christ" and "Messiah" are words for the "anointed one," a divine messenger who reflects the cosmic principle of love.

Wendy Goddard

From the point of Light within the Mind of God

Let light stream forth into the minds of men

Let Light descend on Earth.

From the point of Love within the Heart of God

Let love stream forth into the hearts of men.

May Christ return to Earth.

From the centre where the Will of God is known

Let purpose guide the little wills of men-

The purpose which the Masters know and serve.

From the centre which we call the race of men

Let the Plan of Love and Light work out

And may it seal the door where evil dwells.

Let Light and Love and Power restore the Plan on Earth.

Unsurprisingly, they did not manage to get through it all but were helped by my sons, who completed it with

Hold on to what is good even if it is a handful of earth.

Hold on to what you believe even when it is a tree that stands by itself.

Hold on to what you must do even when it is a long way from here.

Handle Gently: An Exploration of a Journey through Grief

Hold on to life even when it is easier letting go.

Hold on to my hand even when I have gone away from you.[7]

Family and friends produced a delicious cream funeral tea at home with cakes, sandwiches, and scones. In the center of the table stood a cake made by my youngest granddaughter and decorated with a large bee in memory of Granddad, the beekeeper. At times like this, you realize that your family is truly grown up and independent and able to provide for you rather than the other way round. Peter would have loved it all: such a fitting tribute to a man who preferred simple, homely things and believed so strongly in family.

Everyone who attended the funeral and the house afterwards signed a commemorative book. Condolence messages, the order of service and my eulogy all went into it. There is his last birthday letter to me, which I found on the computer, and which he had not given me, and there too, his last Valentine's Letter. Peter never believed in sending cards, though he always remembered children's birthdays and, if anything, he was the one who ensured that I would remember all anniversaries.

He had said that few would attend his funeral. How moved he would have been by the number who came and the book full of

---

[7] Alice A. Bailey, The Externalisation of the Hierarchy, pp. 144 - 171; 251 - 283; 488 - 491.

wonderful messages from family and friends far and wide, a great accolade to a man of humility and gentleness.

His influence continued: During the year, I won an award for a local charity I had set up 18 years before and then heard that an article I had written about his last days and the funeral was the winning entry for "I am a Columnist...Get me in Here" in my local paper. He would have been so proud of me, but I have only him to thank. He was the one who always encouraged me to follow whatever my enthusiasms were and wherever they would take me.

On the day he died, my youngest son, a musician, was away at the Southern Lights Festival. He and his friends, who all knew Peter because of our camping weekends together, witnessed a magnificent rainbow, complete and vibrant, shining over the Purbeck hills. One end of it seemed to be right over the spot where Peter had chosen to have his ashes scattered, the last place we had visited together. We believed that this was a sign from him: his final message to us, "You did well!"

Thoughts

1. The funeral is not the hardest part. It is a celebration of a life well lived, and pleasure can be gained from making it so, from listening to and deciding upon the music to choosing the readings. It takes courage to do it yourself but at least it is done the way you want it. It helped me during those last dark days to begin to plan, and I am glad I did because it would have been hard to have done it all during the week following his death.

2. It takes courage too, to read a eulogy for a loved one. But even if the voice quavers and the tears flow, to be able to say a last goodbye is an opportunity not to be missed.

3. Involve the family in the funeral as much as you can however difficult. The children cried while reading the Prayer but this is how it should be. Tears flowing now will lessen the pain for them later.

4. I find it hard to ask for help, but responding to the offers from family, friends, and neighbors was essential. Let them work out ways to help you spare your energy and maintain your balance. But also, by helping, it allows them the opportunity to heal.

Wendy Goddard

Chapter 5 Testing "Cupboarding"

Grief is "the conflicting feeling caused by a change or an end in a familiar pattern or behaviour. The human condition doesn't like change; it rejects change. It wants stasis so it can go back to what it knows."[8]

Over-activity or inertia and fatigue are common symptoms that accompany the grieving process. I found that one minute, I was clearing out cupboards and trying to sort things into wanted and unwanted piles, and the next moment, I would be too tired to put everything back. I would break down into fits of inconsolable tears, and of course, by this time, people had gone on to resume their lives. I was left alone, never for very long, but long enough to feel the emptiness and the despair at not managing my life well.

I spent a month trying to organize and then re-organize things around me. I know that most of this was about trying to rid the house of sickness and indulging in business to avoid facing the reality of

---
[8] Russell Friedman, Grief Recovery Institute

death. I smudged rooms with sage sticks; I chanted and drummed around the house and then began moving pieces of furniture, trying to reclaim parts of the house as my own. I decorated the living room and changed the curtains and furniture. This was not an effort to dispel Peter in any way, but a way of trying to reconnect with normality and a 'life goes on' attitude. It did not last long. As I write this and review those months after he died, I was in a different world. I was trying to make sense of this new world without him.

I realize that my attempts to do the clearing out were thwarted by inertia and by periods of not wanting to change anything. Then, I would be overcome by energy and start again. I was very brave to redecorate when I did, and I find it interesting to review my choice of wallpaper – a big, bold floral one that Peter would not have liked. Of course, that meant changing the curtains, and he would certainly have grumbled about that too, as the ones we had were 'perfectly good'. As I changed them every few years, he always said the same thing. Was this rebellion my way of expressing anger towards him for leaving me? In retrospect, maybe there was a bit of this because now, when I look at the room, I am not even sure I like it so much.

It would be nearly three years before I finally started to clear the lifetime of clutter that filled the house. But in those early days, I made small attempts. Peter was a collector of things. Not of anything valuable but of 'useless' or 'broken' things that 'one day might be needed'. We both kept items we had finished with just in case the children or grandchildren should ever need them, and thus our attic had gradually filled up, as indeed had Peter's big shed in the garden. He was a collector of maps, and there were boxes of them in the attic. There are also photos and records of his life before we met which belong to his family, and I have been postponing going through these.

Thoughts

1. Take things slowly. Do not rush into making big decisions that involve big changes.

2. Learn to sit with these feelings of grief and embrace them as they help you to heal.

3. It really does not matter that I have not cleared all the 'clutter'. I have learned that jobs started do not have to be completed at once. There is a change in the pace of life and what seemed very important actually is not any longer. Three years on, and two of my grandchildren have bought their first homes, so much of what I might have cleared out then may now be useful to them. I can almost hear Peter saying, "I told you not to get rid of that. One of them may want it in the future."

4. However, as the Prayer of Invocation says, "We need to hold on to what we must do even when it is a long way from here." There will come a time when we are ready to move on.

Wendy Goddard

Chapter 6 Still Testing
Running away to the USA

"You can't run away from yourself" Bob Marley

I found a hundred ways to run away from the pain. After settling the accounts, dealing with probate, and my 'Cupboarding' stage, I appended myself to my son's journey in the USA along with my grandchildren.

When looking for ways to deal with (run away from) grief try a holiday, I thought. No, correct that, a camping experience, along with a 46-year-old musician in mid-life crisis searching for meaning; an 18-year-old "modern woman" (gorgeous, glamorous, but no camper!); and a "Bear Grylls" hunk of 21 seeking outward bound bonding experiences with Dad. Throw into this mix a grieving grandmother, unsure of her future, rather unstable on her feet and yearning for quiet places to access solitude for meaningful meditation. Pile them into a Bob Marley campervan (suitable for youthful hippy honeymooners) and set off on the road through America. Two and a half thousand miles travelled in three weeks, with an elder trying to educate a teenager on the early history of the USA - unsuccessfully, as it happens when the said teenager is wired up (headphones in), hooked up (mobile 'Facebook' on) and unplugged from everything around her but shopping and sunbathing.

To say I found peace would be a lie; to admit that it was an illuminating experience would be true; to declare that it was an amazing adventure would be an exaggeration. However, I did find some answers regarding my life. I love my family, but I need to retain my independence; I enjoy making their lives more comfortable in a material sense. However, I learnt that being over-generous can result in expectations and resentment. I exhilarate in the fresh air, campfires and the sense of community to be found on campsites, but I need my home comforts too (wet wipes, wasps and finding toilet blocks in the dark do nothing for me!); I relish silence, and being alone is actually an opportunity to explore new ideas.

I enjoyed being thought of as a wacky senior 'snow bird' especially when seeking provisions from a local store with our Bob Marley painted van parked outside, "Jammin" blaring forth, and a rather startled girl serving me with the items on the shopping list supplied by my crew: "Cigarette papers, cigarettes, tobacco, beer, wine, oh and I guess eggs, butter, bread".

"My, you're quite something, Grandma!" a hick young fella of about 80 said to me with a wink. I assume he thought that I was not only a keen camper but also a smoking alcoholic! I think he was actually looking to hook up with me.

I suddenly felt much older, out of place and out of time, missing the safety of my home and familiar things. Being out of my comfort zone had helped shift things along for me emotionally, but it was so good to return home eventually to a hot bath, a cozy bed and lulled to sleep by Beethoven and Bach.

Bob **was** fun though!

As I write this I remember previous occasions in my life when I have run away. I think it is part of my life style, a way of coping with difficulties. When I was about 13, I attended a Convent School, which I loved. I was always one of the oldest girls as they were beginning to expand from a junior school when I first arrived. So I grew up with the school. The nuns were warm and loving towards us and I was given responsibilities towards the younger children that I enjoyed. I was not very happy at home during the holidays being of that age when mother and daughter did not see eye to eye. One particular summer holiday was exceedingly problematic as my father had gone to London to work and left my mother in charge of the country pub they owned. Without my father there to come between the warring women, things grew to a head, and we had a huge row. I have no doubt that I was challenging her as only teenage girls can, but I was shocked at the verbal violence in that row.

The following morning I rose early, packed my bag and ran away back to school. The convent was about 50 miles away as the crow flies, but at that moment, that was nothing. I hitched lifts where I could and arrived back at the school in time for supper. I was greeted with such warmth by the nuns, who, hearing my story, were very sympathetic. But, of course, told me that I would have to return home after contact was made with my mother. I think my father came down from London to collect me the next day. I remember he used to call the Reverend Mother "Reverend Mum," and maybe he recognized that during those years, she was much more of a mother to me than my own mother.

Another occasion happened in more recent years. I went to a school reunion and met with eight friends from those teenage years. We arranged to stay in the convent, which was no longer run as a school, and we had dinner at a nearby hotel. I did not enjoy the evening. I found I had nothing in common with these 'old friends' and now we were all in our late 50's we had followed quite different paths in life. Listening to the success stories of those who had made wise career choices or were happily married to rich husbands, I missed Peter, my soul mate, and I wanted to be at home with him. So, rather than wait for breakfast to say goodbye, I left a note on the table explaining that I needed to get home and drove away. At least this time, I had a car. The interesting aspect of this escape is that I am still unsure whether I was running away from my childhood, having been given the same bedroom I had slept in as a child, or whether I was running away from the adults my young friends had become. Whatever, these were two difficult circumstances which came to mind when I started to question why I had gone on holiday with the family at this time.

Denial is probably one of the best-known defence mechanisms, used often to describe situations in which we seem unable to face reality or admit an obvious truth. It is an outright refusal to admit or recognize that something has occurred or is currently occurring. Indeed, victims of traumatic events may deny that the event ever occurred. But denial also functions to protect the ego from things that we cannot cope with. While this may save us from anxiety or pain, denial requires a substantial investment of energy. Because of this, other defences are also used to keep these unacceptable feelings from consciousness.

In many cases, there might be overwhelming evidence that something is true, yet we will continue to deny its existence or truth because it is too uncomfortable to face. Denial can involve a total rejection of the existence of a fact or reality. In other cases, it might involve admitting that something is true but minimizing its importance.

I was admitting that Peter had gone and would not be coming back but, at the same time, I was denying the importance of this by trying to find pleasure in travelling without him. The fact that I had chosen to go on a tour of America to places we had visited together only accentuated the fact that he was not beside me. When I returned home, I had to face the emptiness all over again. I had merely postponed the reality of the feeling of desperate loneliness without him. It was as if I had to start the grieving process again. I had to learn to live with the pain until I could accept it.

I realise how much energy I had expended in those first few months trying to escape from this reality. I think this slowed down my recovery. I had busied myself with decorating, clearing out cupboards, spring cleaning and then going on quite an exhausting trip.

Thoughts

1. Running away does not help. Often, we think we are being brave and coping well, and so we make choices that are not honest. I knew deep inside me that the American trip was not right for me then.
2. Being alone is sometimes easier than being lonely in a crowd. I have learnt to enjoy the solitude.
3. Examining past experiences can help to unearth the reasons for present behaviours. Running away was a pattern of behaviour, my life style that I used when I could not cope. I recognise too, that my occasional thoughts of suicide were merely another expression of this behaviour.
4. Hold on to life even when it is easier letting go. This line from the Prayer of Invocation stayed with me throughout. And although I have taken small steps forward and large steps backwards, I know that holding on to the rope of life is so precious. I have hope too that joy will return.

Chapter 7 Moving On
Cat and Clocks

"You will achieve a grand dream, a day at a time, so set goals for each day, not long and difficult projects, but chores that will take you, step by step, toward your rainbow. Write them down, if you must, but limit your list so that you won't have to drag today's undone matters into tomorrow. Remember that you cannot build your pyramid in twenty-four hours. Be patient. Never allow your day to become so cluttered that you neglect your most important goal: to do the best you can, enjoy this day, and rest satisfied with what you have accomplished." [9]

I kept finding lists that Peter had made on the backs of envelopes. Some of the jobs would probably get done in due course. Others no longer seem so important. But list making for both of us was, and still is for me, a very valuable exercise. Whenever family members or clients seem overwhelmed by the amount of things they have to do or depressed by life in general, I suggest that list-making is a great remedy. It helps to clarify the mind and put things into perspective. My list was growing daily, and I realized I would have to add his items to it. Things like

---

[9] Og Mandino: A Better Way to Live

updating our address list on the computer, exploring cheaper insurances for when it was time to renew them, the endless decorating jobs, cleaning out the gutters, clearing up the garden, maintaining the car, changing the clocks and so on.

Twice a year, changing the clocks was Peter's job and at the past Winter solstice, I still hadn't got around to doing them all. But I would like to know how Thomas, the cat, still thinks we are in summer time.

Thomas is quite a character. He used to live opposite with a lovely old lady who suffered from Parkinson's disease. Whenever she was taken to the hospital, we fed and watered him, and when she became very poorly, she asked us if we would have Thomas should she be unable to look after him. He was so important to her, not having any family of her own, although he often scratched her. I reasoned that it was probably because he was quite anxious about her jerky movements. Peter was fond of our neighbour and, rather rashly, reassured her that we would. That day came when she finally went into a nursing home.

Thomas packed his bag: one collar, two rugs, two bowls and a brush, and moved in. We did not even have to encourage him. He seemed to know that she would not return, and having often been over the road to visit us, he decided the time had come to relocate. He made himself quite at home. He is a very large Felix-type cat with a smart tuxedo coat and one white paw. He is highly intelligent and talks incessantly, never failing to greet anyone when they enter the house and leaving the room when those who do not like cats appear. My husband used to have long conversations with him. But I tend to ignore him, and he responds by bopping me round the legs as I walk past him. He doesn't like to be ignored. But he doesn't do laps either, so it is like having another man around the house..... Give him water, food, a place to sleep and listen to his moans, but don't expect too much demonstrative affection in return.

He would make a great office cat if I could train him to press the right keys on the computer, but unfortunately he tends to sit on the keyboard at inopportune moments and I find he has made nonsense of my documents. Worse still, he invariably fires off an email with rubbish on it.

However, he was canny enough to be the first to know that Peter was seriously ill. He started to follow his nose to heel around the house, sat on his lap, and generally gave him more attention than was normal. We laughed it off until the doctors revealed the truth. Since then, I have been a little more tolerant of his funny ways. Although I do get rather concerned when he follows me around, I think he is just getting used to having me for company, as we both grow old together.

But back to my question. How do you tell a cat that it is too early for breakfast? He has taken to knocking things down my wooden stairs to wake me up, picking a fight with the cat next door through the cat flap so that it bangs incessantly while they yowl at each other for about 10 minutes; he is far too cowardly to go out outside and face the neighbor, cat to cat. More recently he has started jumping on top of me and padding on my chest whilst meowing in my face. So either he thinks it is still Summer time, or he knows that I need a reason to get up.

I think I had better put all the clocks back in case he can tell the time, and then maybe I can benefit from the extra hour.

Whilst doing this I realized the grandfather clock had stopped at more or less the time that Peter died. I still haven't been able to start it up again.

Peter was my instrument that kept me connected, synchronized and attuned to the world and when his heart stopped my rhythm ceased.

Thoughts

1. If you make lists each day it helps to gain afresh that feeling of achievement. If there are only two or three items to be done, then that is okay.
2. Animals help. Caring for their needs can bring you out of yourself when you only want to shut yourself away or stay in bed. Most of all they make you laugh with their funny ways.
3. I need to find a different rhythm from the one we shared.

Wendy Goddard

Chapter 8 Depression
Grief Encounter – A Love Letter

Take my hand quick and tell me,
What have you in your heart?
Speak now, and I will answer;
How shall I help you, say;
Ere to the wind's twelve quarters
I take my endless way.[10]

Just as I thought I was getting on with life, doing the jobs that have piled up, seeing friends I have neglected, getting back into theatre outings and immersing myself into the flow of work, the emptiness hits me. Peter is no longer here to laugh with me over those idiot moments of the day, to discuss events in the news, to share decisions about decorating, and to face the highs and lows of life together. As we once stood united against the world, now I am alone. I used to love that feeling that whatever happened, he was always in my corner. Now he is gone, and he is never coming back. Five months later, the reality hits home again, and I feel I am

---

[10] A.E.Houseman (1859 -1936) A Shropshire Lad XXXI1

fragmenting. I am faced once more with the finality of the loss. Nothing I can say or do will ever bring him back.

I was the one who always wanted to be in control - Peter, the one who let me be, supported me and allowed me to organize our lives. How am I to survive without him? This is the one part of my life I cannot control... losing him. I relive the moments he lay dying in my arms, and they blot out the happy memories. I feel as though I am losing him every night when I awake from dreams of him, and during the day, I cry in his absence.

Words of comfort are meaningless: "This will pass", "Think of the happy times", "You are strong", and that really strange sentence: "At least you had time to prepare for his passing". One can never be prepared! Rationally, I know this will pass, that I will be able to survive, that I will be able to reminisce on happier days. But right now, in this dark place, I feel lonely, vulnerable, scared and lost.

But it is OK to admit that and hear myself say that aloud. He always said that I spoke for others when they could not find the words. Now, I need to speak this anguish aloud for myself.

Maybe then others who may read this and are experiencing this too will somehow feel comforted by the fact that we do have the right to grieve, to take our time with it for as long as it takes, to shut the world out so that we can feel our loss; to reach out when we are ready and know there are ears to listen, hands to grasp and hearts to care. We all grieve in different ways and there is no wrong or right way.

There is comfort in knowing that: "So long as men can breathe, or eyes can see, So long lives this, and this gives life to thee."[11]

I read his letters to me over and over again as if to remind myself that I was once loved so. It hurts, but I need to stay with the pain. To really feel it so that the light can eventually begin to shine through again.

Peter wrote in a Valentine Letter:

"I am incapable of managing a home that's fit to live in; or deciding which car to buy or which insurance to choose. As for cooking a meal alone... but that is not why I can't imagine what it would be like if you were no longer here and I were left on my own... I told you when we were first together that I felt happier than I have ever been...and I still am... I love you like a swan, as a mate for life. I want to be with you always and to protect you. I hope and expect to be with you until the end. I rely on you. You are my best friend, as you have always known: my only real friend. I look forward to the happiness of the next decade and a half and to all the things we are going to enjoy doing together, my love."

---

[11] William Shakespeare – Sonnets Shall I compare Thee

We never got that decade and a half, but we got a few of those years together. Reading this letter, I feel that in many ways, it is fortunate that he died first because I think he would not survived so well on his own. He would have coped, but he would have suffered and I would not want that to have happened for him.

Thoughts

1. Read those letters and stay in the moments they illuminate. I find that they are a comfort in the dark times.
2. Ignore the comments people make. Some will find it hard to find the right words; others who are grieving often lash out with meaningless sayings because they are defending their pain.
3. Accept that just when you think everything is getting better, you will be kicked in the gut yet again by heart-breaking pain. But it will pass. And each time you rise from it, you will be stronger.
4. Sometimes I fear that I am being self-indulgent and wallowing in my grief, but I honestly feel that we need to be true to ourselves and if the pain hits us and life seems hopeless again, then we need to be able to stay with the feeling in order to feel the joy again.

Chapter 9 Longing – Yearning

"Give me the waters of Lethe that numb the heart, if they exist, I will still not have the power to forget you."[12]

It is a Sunday, and I am alone. I do not want to do anything or go anywhere. I look at his photo and feel such a deep sadness and longing that the tears well up inside me and break like water over a dam.

I miss the way he made me smile when the day seemed dark. I miss the way he said my body was beautiful to him. I miss the way he held my hand as we walked along the beach. I miss the way he would take risks and yet make me feel so safe. I miss the way he kissed me like a hesitant lover, not sure how to do it. I miss the way he would lie with me, his body wrapped around me and his arms enfolding me spoon-like, protecting me from harm.

There are certain life events that seem to destroy the personality. "Shattered" is a good word to describe what I feel right now. I feel as though I have dissolved into a myriad of particles, each piece

---

[12] Ovid, The Poems of Exile: Tristia and the Black Sea Letters

representing a part of myself that has been lost in my desperately damaged psyche.

So I seek sleep, which does not come easily, and my hours of night turn into wakeful ones, and the daylight hours become sleep filled. I dream a lot, and more than that, I seek out these dreams, desperately trying to hang on to them and analyze them because I feel they are paving the way for the construction of a new integrated self.

I keep going back through my memories to find that resilient core within me that I can build upon and learn from. But it is hard to find at times. I know that basically I am strong and able to withstand the "slings and arrows", but oh, how tempting it sometimes seems to "end the heartache".

And so each day, there is a battle to survive the pain, a pain that has moved from the emotional depth of longing to a physical pain in my back and my legs, one unable to bear the weight, the other unable to move me forward.

I have headaches; sometimes I find myself trembling for no reason; uneasy palpitations occur in the night, and several times, especially when venturing out, I have had an upset stomach. I am reminded of PTSD and so begin to wonder if I have gone into shock. My inability to get moving is like a shutting down: a not unheard of response to an unbearable situation. Like a deer in the headlights, I am caught in this glaring spotlight of grief.

Handle Gently: *An Exploration of a Journey through Grief*

Among the list of attributes given to neurosis I find the following all of which apply to me at this time: anxiety, sadness, irritability, lack of confidence; avoidance of situations involving people, extra vigilance at night, lethargy, unpleasant or disturbing thoughts related to Peter's dying, and negative thinking. And yet, as I write this, I feel angry with myself. I feel that I am letting myself down. I am ashamed that I am finding it hard to cope. There is a small voice inside me that is telling me that I need to stand tall, shoulder the grief and fight on. And of course, I will...

I am still trying to find that wonderful state where I can become totally absorbed in something so that I lose all track of time. The psychologist Mihaly Csikszentmihalyi calls this state of mind 'flow', and there's a huge amount to be said for it. It takes away all care and introspection. It is neither a state of happiness or excitement. It has no distractions of emotions. It is a state that I can normally get into when working, writing or doing something I enjoy, like reading. But even that is proving elusive at the moment. I find that I read a paragraph and have to re-read it because my mind has wandered. Or I start to work and flit from one task to another. Or worse still I find my usual ability to meditate is being disrupted by thoughts of Peter and his last days. My thoughts 'are all a case of knives, wounding my heart.'[13]

---

[13] George Herbert - Affliction

Wendy Goddard

At the weekend my family took me out on the water to watch the birds in Poole harbor. The boat took us round the islands for a couple of hours and for the first time I began to relax and let my mind empty, not just watching the birds but watching the sea. There is something so hypnotic about the rhythm of the waves and the gentle movement of the boat that I felt lulled into a very calm state of mind.

I felt the parts of me that were 'broken in pieces all asunder' were beginning to come together and then breaking again like the white horses on top of the waves. I realized that this aching and hurting was all part of me. There would be days when I would be calm and other days when I would feel like the rough sea, stormy, destructive and grey. But just as spring comes after the cold and dark of winter, so too shall come my renewal.

I had a dream a few nights ago. My son was standing on an ice flow with his dog. I could not reach him from where I was on a raft, and I was leaning out stretching my hands to him. Finally I jumped, no fell, into the sea. I swam towards where I thought he was but instead, the iceberg gradually moved over me and I was submerged beneath the shallow part of it. I could see the blue of the sky and the darker blue of the sea but I knew somehow I was stuck beneath it. I did not panic. I felt calm, peaceful, quiet. What did this mean? My son was not alone; he had his dog and others with him. I couldn't reach him from where I was and though I tried, I was quite calm as

I lay beneath the iceberg. Maybe this is about acceptance. Acceptance of this place I am in. It is different from being with others, detached, still, but calm and peaceful.

In the "Dark Night of the Soul", Thomas More speaks of Jonah and how being in the whale's belly is like a kind of womb. I find this idea of withdrawal from life and the uncertainty I feel at the moment is now somehow comforting......a process like birth or in this case, rebirth. A time of waiting and trusting, sitting with where I am, like the client on a therapist's couch, feeling the moment.

Thoughts

1. I realize that I have changed. Where before I was very gregarious I have become more comfortable with solitude. This is a good place to be. I do not get lonely even though at times, I do experience that loss of my soul mate. I acknowledge now that I was alone for many years before he came into my life and can be so again.

2. Writing dreams down helps to sort out what is happening in our thoughts and emotions. It is only by acknowledging these feelings can we learn to deal with them. And the dreams may be saying something important in our unconscious state. May even be guiding us in a direction we had not thought of before.

Handle Gently: An Exploration of a Journey through Grief

Chapter 10 Acceptance?
Festive Merriment!

I think there must be something wrong with me, Linus. Christmas is coming, but I'm not happy. I don't feel the way I'm supposed to feel. I just don't understand Christmas, I guess. I like getting presents and sending Christmas cards, and decorating trees and all that, but I'm still not happy. I always end up feeling depressed. -Charlie Brown

Festive merriment! Bah, humbug!

When Peter was alive, he always thought I overdid Christmas. Now he has gone I feel I don't want to do it at all. The shops are full of gifts that no one really wants, the decorations and lights seem such a waste of money in this time of austerity, and the family is all spread about the world this year. So, for once I am going to go along with Peter's views and cancel it.

One of the memorable Christmas days we had together was in a year when the family was busy with other things. We spent the day alone watching "Gone with the Wind" all afternoon, and in the evening we had a special meal for two, from a local superstore, which didn't need much preparation. It was lovely and I look back with great comfort on that day we had together.

Alternate years we would go off travelling so that our married children did not have to feel divided between the families. A memorable Christmas was spent on a rice boat in the middle of a lagoon in Cochin being served a wonderful goat curry on banana leaves by a very polite non-English-speaking chef. We were two passengers on a converted barge made for four with our own chef and cabin wallah. I remember Christmas night; the full moon was reflected on the water and the stars shone as brightly as I have ever seen. Not only romantic but a moment in our history book together.

Another year, we went to Australia and spent Christmas on the Murray River with my brother and his family. Strange to be so hot at that time of year and we enjoyed swimming in the river, outdoor barbeques and warm evenings. But how we longed for our own family and snow on the fields.

Somehow sharing the Christmas spirit of tinsel and holly and turkey and trimmings is impossible when the only person in the world I really want to share it with is no longer with me?

As the first frosts and snows of winter arrive and darkness spreads over the land, it seems this is the time of withdrawal. We turn inwards literally and metaphorically. We light candles in remembrance of the Light that has gone and in hope for the Light that is to come. I am going to use this time for reflection and growth, and hopefully, by the New Year will have some sense of who I am now without Peter in my life.

In the end, it was a wonderful Christmas. I spent some time volunteering, driving elderly people to an evening service and Christmas Day was spent in a derelict stable in the Purbecks. What better place could we have found? We had a wonderfully simple meal prepared by my eldest son's partner and we sat on picnic chairs surrounded by straw and the song of birds. It was a surreal experience. The meal was so lovingly prepared and very much enjoyed as we sat with the cold winter sun streaming through the door, warmed by hot soup and wine. Peter would have enjoyed that Christmas. The pain caused by his absence was eased by the fact that the rest of the family was in Peru doing volunteer work. So we three and two friends whose families were also abroad toasted absent family and friends with tears and laughter. This was a memorable Christmas, after all, not least because of the love and care that my son had put into it to help me through.

Thoughts

1. Even the most difficult times can be lightened by the love of family and friends. At times like this it is probably best to ensure you are not alone.
2. There are always people who need comfort at Christmas, and by helping them, I felt warmed by their stories and their gratitude.

Handle Gently: An Exploration of a Journey through Grief

Chapter 11 Disorganization and Despair

Out flew the web and floated wide;
The mirror crack'd from side to side;
"The curse is come upon me," cried
The Lady of Shalott.[14]

I think during the last months, I have been experiencing those cognitive manifestations of grief, including a sense of depersonalization in which nothing seems real, a sense of disbelief and confusion, and an inability to concentrate or focus. I have been preoccupied with images or memories of the loss and dreaming of Peter or sensing his presence.

I have felt as though I am viewing the world through a veil. I do not want to enter it but observe from afar the people and events that cross my path. I am content to let time pass while I spend days half completing mindless tasks. In my mind's mirror, I see "shadows of the world", occasionally wanting to join in but having neither the energy nor the excitement to maintain a pretence of enjoyment. I dip

---

[14] Tennyson - The Lady of Shalott

my toe in a swim at the gym or an evening with the choir, only to find I feel more alone and more unsettled on my return.

I play with ideas in my head. I want to be creative, to weave a 'magic web' and find my song which will lead me back to the rhythm of life, but for the moment, I am content to be isolated from the activity of living.

I find myself wanting to make a quilt. A memorial quilt, a quilt of comfort, which I can wrap around me now that I no longer have Peter's arms to hold me. Much like the 'magic web', which protects the Lady of Shalott from the curse of death, maybe my quilt will protect me from the curse of despair, which is a form of death.

Trying to return too soon into the world has cracked my internal mirror 'from side to side', and I can feel the breaking apart of my life, which once made sense to me.

But hidden within me is the knowledge that everything in life has meaning, and it is up to me to find that meaning in my darkness. And just as Oscar Wilde found humility when he was imprisoned, that "something hidden away in my nature, like a treasure in a field," I have found "vulnerability" in my own imprisonment of grief.

"It is the last thing left in me, and the best: the ultimate discovery at which I have arrived, the starting point for a fresh development. It has come to me right out of myself, so I know that it has come at the proper time. It could not have come before, nor later. Had anyone told me of it, I would have rejected it. Had it been brought

to me, I would have refused it. As I found it, I want to keep it. I must do so. It is the one thing in it the elements of life, of a new life, VITA NUOVA, for me. Of all things, it is the strangest. One cannot acquire it except by surrendering everything that one has. It is only when one has lost all things, that one knows that one possesses it."[15]

I welcome this feeling of vulnerability. I no longer have to prove I am strong. It is all right for me to accept this wounded soul now and to nurture it back to life and strength. Although "I am half sick of shadows", I can also see that this veil is protecting me. It will fade, as I grow stronger.

---

[15] Oscar Wilde - De Profundis

Thoughts

1. This feeling of living in an unreal world is quite common, apparently. Perhaps living veiled from reality is a coping mechanism the self uses.
2. Writing helps, as does finding someone who understands, who can really listen without judgment and without trying to make things better.
3. I think it is time to start a project. You could say that this journal is developing into a project and that when it is complete and I am restored it may give birth to a book which will help others. But I also feel the need to create a practical project.

Chapter 12 Birthday wishes

I do not want much of a present, anyway, this year. After all, I am alive only by accident.[16]

I found last year's birthday card Peter gave to me, the writing so unlike his. I recognize the effort it must have taken him to pen words of love to one he knew he was leaving behind. He never gave me cards, but always wrote me love letters on special occasions and yet this time he must have asked someone to get the card for him, and then he had carefully written: "really love to Wendy, from Peter". It does not make sense but the heart was there in the words. The strange thing is that I do not even remember him giving it to me.

I keep trying to remember what it what was like last year, what we were doing, how he really was, what we talked about, and where we went. I wish that I had kept a better journal of those last months of the good hours we had, not just the diary of doctor's appointments and blood transfusions, temperature and food charts.

---

[16] Sylvia Plath "Birthday Present"

Wendy Goddard

How did we spend his birthday? How did he feel knowing it was his last? Why did we never talk about that?

It is nine months since he died. It seems like yesterday that he asked me to kiss him for the last time. I remember so clearly that as I stopped reading to him and asked him if he wanted anything before going to sleep he said: "Kiss me", and I gently kissed his lips and stroked his forehead. He said: "Kiss me again" and then closed his eyes. Those were the last words he spoke to me in love. Later that night, when he tried so hard to get out of bed and I had to restrain him to prevent him from falling, he said, "You are so strong, Wendy!" but even then, the words weren't said in anger. Those last struggles when the brain refuses to accept the weakness of the body were almost unbearable. When he eventually relaxed and lay down, I knew that was the last time we would have any real connection.

Birthday Poem to Peter

There is never an hour when my thoughts don't drift to you

You fill my mind with the gentleness of you

Your touch lit my soul,

Your smile gave me strength

Your eyes shone with hope

Promising things, you would help me reach.

I dream of places we discovered

Handle Gently: An Exploration of a Journey through Grief

Of distant journeys overseas and mountains

Far off adventures with you beside me.

There is not a breath I take that is not filled with the essence of you

Keeping me alive without you.

Your voice which once filled my heart

Is now silent.

It speaks no more of things to be.

I listen in the void for some sweet word of love

Or look for signs that you still wander close by me

But like a love song, our song has ended

Leaving me with an echo of the refrain.

So many birthday memories we shared when I drove Peter up to the Kimmeridge campsite on his last birthday so that he could say goodbye to all the friends we had made when we sang songs round the campfire.

Or long ago when we celebrated my grandson's birthday with a pink party. He was a small boy of four or five, and he loved the color pink. Everyone had to come dressed in pink; the cake was pink, and the balloons were pink. A couple of years later, he wanted a birthday up on the hills in the outdoors with everyone in army camouflage playing with soldiers. He cried all through his party. I cannot remember why.

We recalled Peter's 70th Birthday spent in a cavers' hut in Cheddar when he took the children caving. How wonderfully brave they all were, even my youngest granddaughter, no more than six at the time! I can remember the little helmeted heads, led by the littlest one, popping up out of the hole where I was waiting for them with tea and sandwiches. They were all a little overcome with what they had achieved but fearful too, particularly as they recounted how grandpa had got lost and the little one had nearly fallen down a crevice. Would they do it again? No way!

For my 50th birthday, Peter had invited all my friends to a surprise party held in the place where we had celebrated our wedding. He had been through my address book, not knowing that this also included ex-boyfriends from many years before and friends that I had 'lost' along the way. We laughed when we thought about how surprised they must have been to receive the invitation. But the ex-boyfriends were kind enough to send good wishes and decent enough not to attend.

Thoughts

1. The memories are to be treasured. Do not be afraid of going through the photos and celebrating them again in your thoughts. There will be new ones to make.
2. Family and friends do understand if you do not want to celebrate annual occasions in the usual way and perhaps finding different ways to celebrate will be fun.

Wendy Goddard

Chapter 13 Sometime in

*When to the sessions of sweet silent thought
I summon up remembrance of things past,
I sigh the lack of many a thing I sought,
And with old woes new wail my dear time's waste.*[17]

Looking back to Christmas, I realize I went through it all in a state of numbness. I accepted whatever my son planned for me and just got through it. This year has been even more difficult. It has been a year of total numbness. The time has passed, and I cannot recall anything of any real significance in it. Nothing seems important any more. I go through the motions of living, working, and filling each day, but I have more empty days when it is hard to get out of bed, let alone actually do anything. I alternate between depression and euphoria, between sobbing and passive resignation. My energy levels are constantly low as though I am bordering on flu all the time. I feel as though I am encased in that iceberg that I dreamt of months ago. I cannot really connect with anyone. I make decisions and then regret them. I have withdrawn

---

[17] William Shakespeare - Sonnets

from friends because I cannot really make the effort to keep them going.

The little things like posting a letter, even getting dressed, let alone driving a car, leave me exhausted. So often I return from the shops, having deserted my trolley in the aisle or not even having got out of the car. I know that this is normal and that by jumping in too soon last year, I have postponed this stage of healing. I know too, that I need to lower my expectations of myself, not beat myself up about reading a book in bed instead of getting on with the day. But then I hear this voice in my head, which tells me it is over a year now, and I should be recovering. But grief doesn't have a time limit or a schedule to stick to. It comes and goes in great waves, and in those tumultuous seas, I flap around like an exhausted fish trying to breathe but unable to swim.

Instead of giving myself time to withdraw and heal I had filled my time with new activities: joining a choir, a book club, a theatre group, and returning to work. Now, this numbness seems to have returned with a vengeance, and for some time, I could not write. I have left the choir and the book club. The first because I found I was not really connecting with the people and the second because I could not always read the chosen book. I do not view either of these as failures to get on with life. They served a purpose for a while, and in retrospect I am surprised that I was even able to join in a concert performance at Christmas. But although singing is a joyous activity, I do not have a voice that adds anything to the choir!

Wendy Goddard

I have cut back on my work, which is a good thing as I feel I can perhaps explore other activities. The theatre club has been a lifesaver because it takes so little effort for a great deal of enjoyment. I am taken by the coach to wherever the play is being performed and returned afterwards. I can converse with like-minded people about the production and join a small group for lunch or go off on my own.

The first time I went, I met with two other widows who seemed very bright and merry. They had lost their husbands fairly recently but did not seem to be grieving. In fact, both said they felt they had got a new lease of life. How I envied them this feeling, at the same time recognizing that they may well be covering up their real feelings just as I was trying to do. We three merry widows wear our masks well, I thought.

The anniversary of Peter's death came around, and I made plans for the future. I bought a little campervan and planned wonderful excursions to Spain and Europe and around Britain. But, as I write this I have to say that my travelling far and wide has not yet happened. I ache with longing for my travelling companion. I cannot imagine journeying without him by my side. But the campervan sits outside, patiently awaiting the planned excursions. I will know when I am ready to go. Meanwhile, the summer beckons, and I will be able to enjoy the camping trips in the Purbecks with the family. At least I will be in comfort rather than in a tent.

Thoughts

1. I don't actually have to achieve anything. Many years ago, someone said to me I was always "doing" and should learn to "be". Maybe this now is the time to "be".

2. Everyone grieves differently. Just as people tell me I am coping well that is what they see because that is all I let them see. Others in grief are probably doing the same thing. Hiding the pain from public view.

3. Finding one activity that is social and enjoyable may lead to others but will at least keep you connected.

Wendy Goddard

Chapter 14 Reorganization and Recovery
Another Year, Another Anniversary

Break, break, break,
On thy cold gray stones, O Sea!
And I would that my tongue could utter
The thoughts that arise in me.[18]

Two years have passed since Peter died. It seems incredible and feels as though the clock is rushing forward towards the end. Time has slipped away and in some ways, I feel as though I have been marking time till my own death. I look back over the past year and find that some days have been well spent, and I have been content, but other days, I have let things slide. I convince myself that it doesn't matter if I have a duvet day, but I feel guilty for the time I am wasting knowing that every day is precious. I know I should get exercise and fresh air and immerse myself in nature, but my motivation and energy are still way down.

---

[18] Alfred Lord Tennyson

Yet, when I look back over the past year, I realize I have functioned reasonably well in certain periods. I have continued to provide supervision for others; I have completed five days of training for the local Council with my colleague; I have provided workshops around the country and at a local Children's Centre; and managed to do the Summer Schools as usual in England and Ireland. So, in many ways, I am still making connections and contributing to the therapeutic community.

But on this day, the second anniversary of Peter's death, I miss him as much as ever. I think about him constantly, and he comes to me in my dreams. When I awake, I have to mourn the loss all over again. It feels as though the best part of me is gone.

Freud believed that, in grief, the world *looks* poor and empty, while in depression, the person *feels* poor and empty. I think that one can veer between these two. Some days, it is the world that seems empty and meaningless without Peter, and on other days I feel that I have lost confidence in myself. I do not know who I am any more or who I want to be. I try to find meaning in my life. I begin to make plans and long lists, but then they get shelved.

I think it is crucial to understand that all these strong feelings will occur, and so will the ambivalence that goes with them. I know that I have to keep them in perspective and to try to understand why I am feeling a certain way at a certain time. I try to make links and look at patterns; sometimes, I see connections with an event or remark. What I find most difficult is the constant feeling of anxiety that accompanies me when I go out or before I am going to do something out of my comfort zone. This emotion seems to mirror the feeling of premonition I used to describe to Peter when I awoke some mornings. He would listen as I went through the fears that I had and in the end, it would normally dissipate. But now he is not there to talk to so the feeling seems to intensify.

I do not feel that I have been able to quite put a closure on the life we shared together. But I am working towards it. I need to find a fresh perspective on life and have a place in it for Peter as a beloved memory.

And so I move into the third year without him, and I am taken by surprise that he has been gone so long.

I am reminded of the time I was about to sit my finals at University, and for the third time in my life, my back gave out on me and I was left in terrible pain and had to lie flat on my back. Having to travel from Sussex to London in order to 'sit' my finals, I realized that I would be unable to do this without help. There was no way I was going to miss them after years of study. I had two small sons to support and had planned to take up teaching when I qualified.

So I rang a friend for help, and he commandeered the support of the local Lions Club. Within a matter of hours, all was organized for the following day. The doctor approved the plans and the College had made their arrangements for me. A 'hearse' arrived the following morning at 6 a.m., hired by the local lads. They lifted my stretcher into the back and drove me to London. On arrival, some hefty male students helped the driver to carry me into the sanatorium, where I was placed gently onto my bed, which was to be my examination desk for the next three weeks. A carpenter friend had rigged me up with an upright table that sat across my chest, and my father had given me a lovely pen that wrote upside down, designed by NASA for space travellers. The examiner sat by my bed, which was very unnerving. At the end of each day, the drivers took me home, where I was able to prepare for the next day.

Looking back at this time, I wonder how I got through it. Without a wonderful team of family, friends and strangers who provided for my needs, I would not have been able to get my degree. Somehow, the strong painkillers did not affect my ability to remember what I had learned. And through it all, I found the courage to continue.

I needed to call on that courage now. After all, I must have it in me, even though it may not be quite as strong as when I was young.

Thoughts

1. All obstacles can be overcome with persistence and courage to face the reality of the situation.

2. Without the help of others, it may be hard to find the answers, but help has to be asked for when needed. People are not mind readers.

3. It helps to recall times when you have overcome the odds. Within those experiences will be the resilience that is needed at this time.

Handle Gently: An Exploration of a Journey through Grief

Chapter 15 Searching for Meaning

Oh, don't you see
That lonesome dove
Sitting on an ivy tree
She's weeping for
Her own true love
As I shall weep for mine
Oh come ye back
My own true love
And stay a while with me
If I had a friend
All on this earth
You've been a friend to me.[19]

A dear friend has just lost her husband. He died peacefully at home surrounded by his family. His name was Peter also, and I have been fortunate to be able to support her through his illness. I know that when we suffer in life that suffering can be turned around to help others. Because I had had to cope with all the practical details like claiming a carer's

---

[19] Mary Chapin Carpenter " 10,000 miles"

allowance and dealing with Peter's pensions and probate, I could provide a practical guide for my friend telling her what needed to be done. I shared with her some of my journals at certain points of her grieving, and she said that it had helped to know that what she was experiencing was not 'madness'.

After I left her on a quiet autumn sunshiny morning, I heard the song '10,000 Miles' sung by Mary Chapin Carpenter on the radio, and I dissolved into tears. What and who was I weeping for now? My friend, her husband, or myself? I realize that grief takes you in the most unexpected moments. I have not cried for quite a while and yet here I was sobbing again for the absence of my love. I came home to an empty house and had no one with whom to share my feelings about my friend and her Peter.

The year has been a difficult one. My health has suffered from my mental distress. I do not seem to be able to get beyond that state of longing for what has gone. I am still searching for meaning in my life. I feel I need to get out there and do something with or for others and yet I keep to my comfort zone.

Interestingly, my sight has suffered and an operation for glaucoma was necessary. I wonder whether this has also been about seeing the world through a veil. And once again I experience a physical lack of balance – just as my life also feels out of balance. The life aspects of relationships, environment, spirituality, work and leisure are out of kilter. I have let relationships with friends wither;

my environment is cluttered and full of items I need to dispose of; my meditation, a source of quiet contemplation for me, has been difficult, as has my relationship with the natural world; exercise has been minimal and work has diminished. So now, with another Christmas and New Year upon me, I need to make plans once again and maybe follow some of them through this year.

Thoughts

1. This New Year is the time to move on so I begin it with a list of things to do in the next few months. I do not feel annoyed with myself that I have not done all those things I planned last year. I have learned to be more patient with myself.

Chapter 16 Anger (2)
Ghosts in the Basement

For last year's words belong to last year's language and next year's words await another voice. And to make an end is to make a beginning.[20]

I had returned one year from a wonderful week at my Adlerian Summer School to find our basement flooded.

It is a lovely basement and we practically lived in it because it leads onto our conservatory and garden. The bedroom, bathroom and library/den can be shut off from the rest of the house so it becomes a sanctuary.

Many years ago we had converted the cellar into this lovely retreat more or less with our bare hands. My youngest son had built beautiful fitted cupboards and shelving and a magnificent floor to ceiling bookcase in oak. It became a very special place and feels a part of me, of who I am. My sons had provided me with a beautiful sanctuary and it represented their wonderful craftsmanship.

---

[20] T.S.Eliot

But my sanctuary was destroyed not merely by the torrential rains that swept through Dorset but by my neighbour's collapsed drains. This was 'dirty' water, contaminated by their sewage and by their negative vibes following the event. They not only got angry and abusive at the suggestion that it might be their drain, but they have not really spoken to us since their drains failed a test and had to be repaired.

I felt sick at heart. My new travertine-tiled bathroom had to be stripped out entirely; the beautiful handmade cupboards taken out from my freshly decorated bedroom and the den had to be totally stripped and refurbished. Moving and storing the books alone was a mammoth task.

I have never been good at dealing with the mess around me. Before I start work, everything has to be in order and with chaos, I cannot function. I was crying all the time and not sleeping. The stress caused not just by the chaos in the basement but by the insurance company, which was refusing some of the liability, as well as by the difficult neighbours, led to my being quite depressed for a while.

And thus had to begin a healing process.

I shut the door to the basement and began every day with a meditation upon good fortune since I do still have a home upstairs; I accepted that the neighbours wish to distance themselves from the event and us and let my anger motivate me into dealing with the insurance company and getting the basement repaired. Most of all I turned to my supervisor to help me deal with my state of mind so that I could continue to work. It was she who first raised the matter of the 'ghosts in the attic'. This was my personal reflection upon this theme.

My supervisor talked about the unwelcome ghosts like uninvited guests at the christening or wedding that, most of the time we banish to a subterranean dwelling place...the basement. We weave a magic circle around them, and they can't get out. However, in an unguarded moment, even in the happiest of places, they break out, and there is a brief intrusion, which means we find ourselves re-enacting a scene from another time and place until we realise what they have done and re-banish them.

This was indeed food for thought. I know my reactions to this disaster (and for me, it was indeed a trauma) were shaped by my own personal story and by the broader cultural and historical narratives that inform my identity, my values, and my sense of place in the world. My home is enormously important to me because I have never really had one for longer than three years. My sons are the most important people in my life, having raised them alone from very early on in their childhood.

When I first bought this house, I had converted the basement. Later, my mother, who had developed Alzheimer's, moved upstairs. The basement became my retreat from her as well as from her illness. The home I created was my testament to the fact that I had overcome those 'ghosts in the nursery' to become the successful, independent woman she had never dreamed I would be. It was also a testament to my sons' talents and with whom I had a bond never possible with my mother. I believe that the figures in my mother's own family had already claimed her unique view of the world; just as her mother had 'given her away', she had never been able to form an attachment with her daughter, only with her sons. She had been abandoned, and so she emotionally 'abandoned' me.

I had banished those 'ancestral' ghosts from my children's nursery as best I could, but they returned to haunt me when I was under stress as indeed they returned to haunt my mother.

But there is something immediate, reflexive and regressive about our encounters with such disastrous events, a turning inward and backward, a sense of primal urgency. We are drawn back into our past, visited by the ghosts of our parents, and haunted by ancient childhood dramas. These visitations and echoes reverberated around the basement, complicating my discussions with family, friends and insurance representatives and filling the space with the voices of people who were not there.

They were beginning to take up residence in my home, not only in the basement, and the more vulnerable I became, the more they troubled me.

Handle Gently: An Exploration of a Journey through Grief

From as far back as I can remember, my mother suffered from bouts of depression, often with attempts at suicide. In fact, she was hospitalised when I was a baby. She often drank heavily and became angry, and this was played out in physical hostility towards me, but mostly, she became verbally offensive. I believe she was the reason we had to move so often in my childhood. She was never content with the lovely homes she created, always wanting something better.

Now here, I was getting depressed, drinking more, feeling angry all the time and preparing to "move" - if only upstairs. Although many times I said I wanted to literally move house and start again afresh. I began to recognise the returning "ghost" accompanied by others in my life who had in some way undermined my identity. These were the other ghosts that had taken up residence and were "conducting the rehearsal of my family tragedy from a tattered script". I began to feel envy towards my brother, who in comparison to me seemed to be wealthy and successful, living in a grand house abroad and building another for himself on a golf course. I began to resent his life, which seemed to me a life of leisure in his comfortable retirement, free from the problems I was facing. Or, thus, it appeared to me at this time. And, of course, this is only my distorted perception of how things are. Childhood ghosts of rival siblings joined the neglectful mothers.

I knew that it would be hard to banish these ghosts, so I started to write down my thoughts about the process. I gave the work back to my sons so that they could rebuild their inheritance! When they sealed the basement from the rest of the house, I smudged and drummed the spirits out! The sunshine meant we could open doors and windows, and because of the penetration of water the whole basement had been stripped back to the brick. It was as though a deep cleansing was taking place.

My anger gradually dissolved, and I became cheerful and optimistic in planning the new decor. I knew that my 'ghosts' were waiting to come back in, but somehow, having my sons and grandson working on rebuilding the basement, the strength and power they carried seemed to overcome that of the ghosts. Every brick they removed to clear away the debris in the cavity walls was replaced, sealing in the cavity all the demons from my past. And my emotional spring clean was completed when celebrated with an opening ceremony.

Then, just before going to the Summer School the following year, my husband died in that basement - our reformed sanctuary. Knowing our time together was limited, we made it such a special time, by cocooning ourselves surrounded by our books, our memories. But, for a while, after he died, the basement seemed again to be haunted by ghosts. Now, two and a half years on, I sometimes awake at night and feel his presence in the next room. Often, I even see his shadow cross the window. I used to wake up calling out to him to check he was all right, but now I know that it is just my longing that causes these aberrations of the senses.

When the New Year started with gales and floods, dark days and long nights, I feared the return of water. I realized, too that what I fear most are the emotions, so hard to contain, that flood my body. I feel that my psyche has been damaged by my grief - old ghosts returning to haunt me. One loss is always hard to bear, but all past losses are added to it like a snowball racing downhill, accumulating snow and growing bigger and bigger until it is so large and heavy it stands still, unable to roll any further. I reflect upon those losses and realize that the only one where my anger seemed able to express itself was when the basement was flooded. The death of a daughter; the destruction of my first marriage; the loss of my health and my teaching career; my mother's Alzheimer's and my father's cancer, which finally took him away; and now this, the greatest loss of all, the death of my soul mate, none of these had caused me to really feel anger. Instead, the anger had been repressed within me, growing through the years, and I can feel it now, and it is beginning to consume me. I have no idea what I am angry about or with whom I am angry, but I recognize the need to feed it. So, my task became one of trying to acknowledge, name, and face it.

In a meditation, it came to me: I had a memory of losing my child and my ex-father-in-law coming to my aid. I had a baby, stillborn, one Saturday afternoon in mid-winter in the flat where we lived above my former husband's shop. He had gone to his rugby, which he played every Saturday. I had begged him not to go because I was in pain, but he ignored my pleas. My father-in-law was downstairs in the shop and heard me cry out and came to help. He called the doctor, but it was too late. My baby had arrived but was dead. When my husband returned late that night, I was angry. I shouted and wept and screamed at him for not being there. He reacted to my anger by pushing me out onto the balcony, which faced the street above the shop. I was only wearing my nightdress. It was Christmas time, and there was a decorated Christmas tree, which we had put on the balcony. The snow was falling and it was bitterly cold, and I hid behind that tree because I was so afraid that someone might see me. I stayed there, silent and shivering from cold and anger, curled up behind the tree until he let me in. From then on, I rarely showed my anger. I became extremely depressed (repressed anger), and it took me a long time to recover. Our marriage lasted another ten years, but the damage had been done, and eventually we parted.

Now, I think that the image of the snowball is quite appropriate. That anger that began in the snow all those winters long ago has, over the years, accumulated with every loss experienced. It is like a huge frozen ball inside me. The work I have to do now is to face that anger and deal with it. I will melt it with the love I have in my life. I will burn candles around my home to dispel the angry ghosts, and

I will light up dark corners at night so that they have no room to hide.

I have mentioned before how chaos in my life disturbs me. Part of that chaos is caused by clutter. I have an attic filled with our past lives, cupboards full of unwanted items, and drawers that need to be sorted. I have had two and a half years to dispose of the clutter and yet have not been able to do this. Now is the time because just like filling my heart with anger leaves no room for love, my houseful of clutter leaves no room for beauty.

This is the time to strip out the old me and start afresh – redecorate and refit- and somehow face life with a different perspective.

Thoughts

1. Anger is often one of the stages of grief. It may not be felt by everyone. It is worth exploring its roots, which may be totally disconnected from the immediate loss.
2. It does not matter how often one makes the decision to turn one's life around. It does not always happen at once. I began to realize that the clutter will be cleared as and when the time is right. And does it really matter that much?
3. The memories that come when searching for connections to past and present are often coloured by our present circumstances. The need to understand why we behave in a certain way is very strong. So I recognise that the perceptions I have of my mother are incomplete. I honour her memory and the struggles she had with her own 'ghosts'

Chapter 17 Acceptance (2)
Time Passes

"I learned that courage was not the absence of fear, but the triumph over it. The brave man is not he who does not feel afraid, but he who conquers that fear."[21]

Nelson Mandela said that, "The greatest glory in living lies not in never falling, but in rising every time we fall." When the great man died, I was conscious of how much he had suffered but had never given up.

Many times over the last months, I felt that I had given up. I have never been a morning person but have always been able to rise at a reasonable hour and get on with the day. When I was teaching, I could awake up at 5 and do my marking and preparation before going to work at 7.30. But at times, it is hard to face a day of what seems to be meaningless activities.

Why is it necessary to clear out the attic? My children will do that when I die. Why do I have to sort out my clothes? I seem to

---

[21] Nelson Mandela

wear the same thing every day and the rest just hang there. I don't like any of them anymore. Why should I take my pills and do my eye drops? I don't really care if I go blind or have a heart attack.

These are the thoughts that go around in my head. They are desperate thoughts and destructive thoughts, and I hate myself for giving in to them. I need the courage to think differently. I need to value myself more as someone who is still capable of contributing to the good of others, connecting with those I cherish, and not giving up.

It is February, the sun is shining, and the daffodils are trying to poke their heads above the sodden earth. After battering winds and weeks of rain, it looks as though the worst of the winter is passing.

I awoke this morning and spent time trying to gauge what I was feeling. I could only imagine myself as a small boat that had been tossed in violent storms for two years and was now becalmed on a flat sea, with no wind to move my sails, no current to sweep me forward. I have felt an absence of energy, an urge to sit and do nothing or take more sleep than I need. I am rudderless, having lost all sense of direction and purpose. I have been driven by winds that have blown me off course and I have followed routes that seemed to have no safe land in sight. Often, I have tired of the journey I have started as soon as I have set out.

I realize that I have a choice: I can bide my time until my demise, or I can start to focus on what I want to do, and if that is to sit and do nothing for a while, that is OK. If I challenge the reality of the last two years since Peter died, I have, in fact, done a great deal. I have continued to write; I have continued seeing my supervisees; I have done some training and been engaged to do more; I go to the theatre regularly and have found new music to enjoy. I have supported my grandchildren through some difficult times and retained my role as an independent and loving matriarch. Over the last few months, I have supported a dear friend through her loss, and now we can give each other support and encouragement.

I do not have to prove anything to anyone, not even to myself. "If nature can handle the destruction and reconstruction of a caterpillar into a butterfly, why shouldn't I surrender and trust that it can handle what is happening to me."[22] I am part of nature, part of that same world that changes the caterpillar into the butterfly and a forest fire into new growth.

I remember when we visited Sydney just after the terrible devastation caused by forest fires. We were amazed to see the buds breaking through the charred forest floor within a week. So, too, I need to begin new growth, and this book has been part of that process. An examination of who I am, where I am going, what I need to change, and to find meaning in the devastation of loss. Finding meaning is about taking back control of my life. Not allowing

---

[22] John Moriarty, Nostos (Dublin: the Lilliput Press 2001) p 53

myself to be buffeted by winds of change but to choose which direction to let myself be blown.

So if I need to stay awhile in this becalmed state and consider these things so be it. It is a quiet place for reflection, for silence. A place to be.

But there are distant shores I see. Lands to be explored.

I must beware of using "the safeguarding devices" which I may be bringing in to protect my self-esteem from the problems of life:

Alfred Adler describes this process of withdrawal: "His retreat is affected by means of his symptoms, and the symptoms are the results of shock effects. These shock effects he has found useful in obtaining relief from a difficult situation. There is no incentive for him to give up the shock effects which have served a purpose for him, so he holds on to them….In this way he builds for himself a narrow stable, closes the door, and spends his life away from the wind, the sunlight and the fresh air!"

I need to turn into the wind, face the sunlight and breathe the fresh air. Maybe I am afraid of moving from my safe place, my familiar territory both physically and mentally, because if I do, I have to face the dangers of that new unknown world that has no Peter in it.

I wrote earlier of my feelings of anxiety, which seem to prevent me from moving forward into a healthier position in my life. I think the state of shock can last a long time. It becomes a sort of frozen state where you can seem to be functioning normally, but in fact, nothing really touches you. The stable gets smaller, and the door harder to open. But I feel with spring approaching there is a new kind of beginning.

Thoughts

1. Self-pity is destructive but part of human frailty. Be kinder to myself and accept those dark nights of the soul as part of the process.
2. It takes courage to live. Having survived until this age has proved that I have the courage within me. I need now to draw upon it.
3. Acceptance. So often, I talk to my clients about acceptance and yet it has been hard to accept who I am now, how I am now, and how I have changed. I have to accept myself in the here and now.
4. Taking time to care for myself emotionally. I spend time sitting watching the birds in the garden, the squirrel knocking down the feeder to get at the nuts, and the flowers beginning to bloom in the early summer sunshine. And this is OK. I do not have to be busy all the time.

Handle Gently: An Exploration of a Journey through Grief

Chapter 18 Becalmed
Three Years On

There are moments when all anxiety and stated toil are becalmed in the infinite leisure and repose of nature.

Henry David Thoreau

Three years, and sometimes it still seems like only a few months ago. I found myself keeping vigil again last night, waking frequently from restless dreams and hearing Peter's voice in my head, "Wake up, Wendy," as he did so often, gently waking me from nightmares.

But I have a task to do. I am going to buy a fig tree and plant it in the garden in memory of Peter. The fig tree seems very appropriate for a man who used to love not wearing clothes. I did some research and found exactly the most suitable type of tree for my garden, one which could survive all winter and be happy in a container.

While I drove around the local nurseries trying to find this elusive tree, I remembered with great joy the times we had laughed at his naturist tendencies. Many years ago we went on holiday with the grandchildren, my son and his wife to Greece. We stayed in a villa near a beach, which was happily unspoilt and very private and Peter spent many happy hours swimming in the nude and lying out on the rocks sunbathing. It wasn't long before the grandchildren followed suit and jumped and skipped in the waves, joyous in their naturalness.

In fact, they loved it so much that I seem to remember one grandson stripping off his clothes at his birthday party, followed by all the other children. I hasten to add that they were no older than four or five at the time. On another occasion, we were at a music festival watching my son's band and suddenly, in front of the entire crowd, this little tot, my youngest granddaughter had taken off her clothes and was dancing totally unselfconsciously in front of the stage. It makes me smile to think about what Peter had started.

Another occasion, I went in search of him at the allotments only to find the shed open, his tools lying around, and his car parked on the verge, but no sign of Peter. I was assured by neighbouring plot-holders that he had been around and as it was so unlike him to leave tools lying about, I assumed he must be there somewhere and began to get concerned. But lo and behold, there he was, lying naked in the sun, hidden among his raspberry canes.

I used to worry when he walked around the house naked in case one day he would forget and open the front door to the friendly

Jehovah's Witnesses who often came to call. I think they enjoyed trying to convert him from Atheism, and he certainly seemed to enjoy debating with them about their theories. However, I am not sure that they would have appreciated his nakedness.

I remembered too how I had bought a new sun lounger for him at the end of year sales so that he would be more comfortable lying in the privacy of the garden the following summer. He never got to use it.

By the time I found the right fig tree, I was in a nostalgic frame of mind, and I told the young assistant why it was so important to me to have found one today. He could not have been more helpful and told me how to take care of it, what soil to use and where to position it. When I got home, I followed his instructions, and it sits now with one small fig on its branches, ready to grow and produce more fruit.

The planting of a tree is a therapeutic event. It needs care and tending so that it can grow and flourish. It also means that there will be a tomorrow.

I have not yet finished the symbolic planting. Although it is now in a new pot, I have some of Peter's ashes to bury in the soil. My son said he would like to put his little pot of the ashes in, too and so together, we will ceremoniously bury the last of his ashes in the fig tree to regenerate life.

Thoughts

1. We can feel so optimistic and full of life one day and yet the next swing back to that place of loneliness and despair. The ever present fear that there is no real purpose in life any more.
2. Focus on the good days. Make plans for the future, however small. Like the fig tree this means we will continue to grow and flourish if carefully tended.

Chapter 19 Moving on

"The whole of human life proceeds along this great line of action -- from below to above, from minus to plus, from defeat to victory. The only individuals who can really meet and master the problems of life, however, are those who show in their striving a tendency to enrich everyone else, those who forge ahead in such a way that others benefit too."[23]

I miss my shelter and my warmth, and I still feel a great wave of emptiness which comes upon me when I realise Peter no longer stands beside me. And then I think how lucky I am to have had such love for so many years. We shared the happiest times of our lives, we withstood tribulations together, and we raised seven wonderful grandchildren, each of them making us proud.

The eighth stage of psychosocial development, where I am now in my 70s, is often termed the stage of Integrity versus Despair.[24] Integrity in old age is the capacity to assimilate the value

---

[23] Alfred Adler (1870-1937), What Life Could Mean to You, 1931/1992, p. 67-68. Translated by Colin Brett.
[24] Erickson 1982

of one's full life experience, to be and to continue to be - through having been - able to hold onto the worthwhile aspects of one's life. These include conscious and unconscious memories of having been valued and loved.[25]

Now is the time for me to begin to assimilate all those rich experiences in order to survive and move forward. The most important of these experiences is the knowledge that I am loved and that I am valued as a mother, grandmother, and teacher. I am now seen as the wise woman, the elder, the matriarch of the family. I feel safe and valued in this place. 'It's clear that at the beginning of a human life and again at the end, love - expressed through delight, gratitude, constancy, interest, good humour, kindness – is what matters most to us.'[26]

The absence of love is something that countless people experience on a daily basis. They may call it loneliness, isolation, dissatisfaction or emptiness. At present, more than half of people over 75 live alone, and a fifth of them report that, on a typical day, they see no one. They have become strangers to love and strangers to themselves. Love joins us to others - we need that - the longing to care for others and be cared for is fundamental to our shared human nature. We are social beings, using our relationships throughout our lives to find out not only what we are capable of giving but also to

---

[25]Martindale 1988
[26] Stephanie Dowrick (2000) 'The Universal Heart'

discover who we are: what makes sense to us, what insight we can achieve, what kind of life we are in the process of creating. Love connects us and inspires us. Our well-being as a society depends absolutely on whether we, as individuals, are willing to care about how life is for other people. Love joins us to the deepest part of ourselves. It allows us to know that our own life has legitimacy, that from our own inner world, we can reach out to give willingly to other people and receive what they can give us.

If we have been lucky to have experienced love and intimacy we are able to continue with open hearts into our later years and share that experience and wisdom gained from it with the younger generation.

I am learning to grow old gracefully. To accept the changes in me and recognise that the passions of my youth are burning out to make room for quiet contemplation of the richness I hope I will leave behind.

I am reminded of the physalis plant, whose fruit is surrounded by an inedible, paper-like husk. As the fruit matures, it fills the husk, and as the fruit ripens, the husk turns into a skeletal structure and holds the new seeds within. I have been the seed and the fruit and am now becoming the husk. When I reach the final state, I will leave behind those seeds, which in turn will leave theirs, and so I live on. But the husk in itself is a thing of beauty, delicate and intricate. And I hope that I will leave a faint, filigree husk of memory, like the beautiful husk I have preserved for many years is just a memory of what it once was and what it contained.

We need others around us to fulfill our potential. Even as we age we need to feel connected to others, to feel capable for as long as we can, to contribute to the well-being of others and to have the courage to keep our spirits high.

"People grow old only by deserting their ideals. Years may wrinkle the skin, but to give up interest wrinkles the soul. You are as young as your faith, as old as your doubt, as young as your self-confidence, as old as your fear, as young as your hope, as old as your despair. In the central place of every heart, there is a recording chamber. So long as it receives messages of beauty, hope, cheer and courage, so long are you young. When your heart is covered with the snows of pessimism and the ice of cynicism, then, and then only, are you grown old. And then, indeed, as the ballad says, you just fade away."[27]

So here I am three years down the road of grief, and I see the rainbow's end. I hope that all those who read this journal are able to reach that place of peace and acceptance where time sometimes can stand still. It has been a very rocky road, and there have been many times when I nearly didn't make it, but with the love and support of family and friends, I am now on a smoother path.

---

[27] General Douglas MacArthur -

I completed a project for my youngest son, a scrapbook filled with photos of his memorable five-week pilgrimage on the Camino de Santiago. He found peace of mind while walking and sharing with fellow travellers. My other son has returned from another winter in Cambodia and is staying with me for the summer. We have developed a rhythm between us that allows independence and connection.

This journal has now served its purpose. I have spent hours writing down my reflections on the road I have had to travel for the last three years. Now, I am at a crossroads. I could travel the same road into the future, gradually becoming quietly reflective and allowing my light to slowly diminish. Or I could take this new road that is opening up before me.

My lifestyle has always been one of fighting back against the knocks that life throws at me. I have overcome some big hurdles along the way, and it seems to me that now, in the twilight years, I should find a way to meet this new challenge head-on and pick myself up to fight another day. It is now about finding what challenges I can face that will keep me connected, capable and contributing to the world around me.

My first challenge will be whether or not to publish. If you are reading this, you will know that after much soul-searching, I am taking the risk. And it is a risk because I know that, in part, I have bared my innermost feelings. But honesty and integrity are the essence of a good therapist, so I do not believe that this short account of life after loss would have been of benefit to myself or to others if I had not been genuine in my struggle.

I have reached that stage where I truly believe that I have turned a corner. I feel more optimistic about planning my future, travelling without my companion, and fulfilling the role of grandparent for us both.

My campervan is ready to take me to far-flung parts of the British Isles to find beauty and peace in nature. Hopefully, like Yeats

I shall have some peace there,

For peace comes dropping slow,

Dropping from the veils of the morning to where the cricket sings;

There midnight's all a glimmer, and noon a purple glow,

And evening full of the linnet's wings.[28]

---

[28] W B Yeats Innisfree

Notes

Wendy Goddard

Notes

Bibliography:

1. Algernon Charles Swinburne
2. Oscar Wilde, De Profundis
3. Author Unknown
4. Oscar Wilde : De Profundis
5. W.H.Auden
6. W.H.Auden
7. Alice A. Bailey, The Externalisation of the Hierarchy, pp. 144 - 171; 251 - 283; 488 - 491.
8. Russell Friedman, Grief Recovery Institute
9. Og Mandino: A Better Way to Live
10. A.E.Houseman (1859 -1936) A Shropshire Lad XXX11
11. William Shakespeare – Sonnets Shall I compare Thee
12. Ovid, The Poems of Exile: Tristia and the Black Sea Letters
13. George Herbert - Affliction
14. Tennyson - The Lady of Shalott
15. Oscar Wilde - De Profundis
16. Sylvia Plath "Birthday Present"
17. William Shakespeare - Sonnets
18. Alfred Lord Tennyson
19. Mary Chapin Carpenter " 10,000 miles"
20. T.S.Eliot
21. Nelson Mandela

22. John Moriarty, Nostos (Dublin: the Lilliput Press 2001) p 53
23. Alfred Adler (1870-1937), What Life Could Mean to You, 1931/1992, p. 67-68. Translated by Colin Brett.
24. Erickson 1982
25. Martindale 1988
26. Stephanie Dowrick (2000) 'The Universal Heart'
27. General Douglas MacArthur -
28. W B Yeats Innisfree

Handle Gently: An Exploration of a Journey through Grief

Reviews

"This moving book has let me reflect on my own journey and each reflection is the opportunity for a healing moment, and therefore acceptance of how things are right now!"

"This is a wonderful book about how the whole being is affected by grief. The author describes brilliantly the physical expressions of raw emotional turmoil. How the brain won't seemingly let you rest or find "flow". Then a moment of space, an inkling that you are still able to lose yourself in something other than thoughts about loss. The description of the sea as the inspiration she needed to realise the impermanence in everything, the ebb and the flow of the water, the seasons and of life was truly magical."

"I love the introduction, it's honest, open and clearly acknowledges the difficult journey the reader will undoubtedly be already on. Particularly poignant that the author, as a seasoned therapist, listening to many others losses, and experiencing other losses already in her life, clearly say this is different and tough.....this has been born out by other people I have spoken to, and its actually quite comforting when you are in overwhelm."

Wendy Goddard

"A lovely reflective chapter where you acknowledge the need for everyone to love and to be loved. You show gratitude for the people who have helped shape you to this point and bring the reader gently to the plateau by which you feel the reflection on your particular grief journey should end."

The writing is flawless and I was moved to tears many times. I really cannot praise your book highly enough - it is a real treasure."

www.ingramcontent.com/pod-product-compliance
Lightning Source LLC
Chambersburg PA
CBHW050252120526
44590CB00016B/2324